Pen-Friends

A Comedy

Ken Whitmore

Samuel French—London
New York – Sydney – Toronto – Hollywood

Please note our NEW ADDRESS:

Samuel French Ltd
52 Fitzroy Street London W1P 6JR
Tel: 01 - 387 9373

PEN-FRIENDS

First presented as a *Saturday Night Theatre* production on BBC Radio 4 in October 1977 with the following cast of characters:

Bethany	Heather Stoney
Hedwig	Carole Hayman
Patrick	Ronald Baddiley
Ted	Christopher Godwin
Kitty	June Barry
Jack	Richard O'Callaghan
Bill	Bob Grant

The play was directed by Alfred Bradley

The action takes place in the drawing-room of a country-house in Cumbria

ACT I

SCENE 1 Mid-afternoon, Friday
SCENE 2 7 p.m. that night

ACT II   10 p.m. that night

Time—the present

To Delia Grözinger,
my German pen-friend

ACT I

SCENE 1

Patrick and Bethany Silverlock's drawing-room. Mid-afternoon on a Friday in midsummer

It is a richly-furnished, country-house drawing-room with oak-panelling and discreet central-heating radiators. A door UC leads to the rest of the house, and there are french windows R and a stone fireplace L. The furniture includes a Chesterfield, a large armchair, two small armchairs, a drinks cabinet, a desk with a telephone, a chair, and two small tables. Paintings and expensive china ornaments are dotted around the room and there is a pair of silver candlesticks on the mantelshelf

Hedwig, a pretty blonde of twenty in a beautiful summer frock enters through the french windows carrying several loaded sprigs of pink may blossom which she has just picked. She looks about for a vase and finally picks up a crystal one containing fresh roses from the small table. After a short debate with herself she removes the roses, goes to the window and dumps them unceremoniously. Then very pleased with herself, she arranges the blossom in the vase

The door opens and Bethany, a woman of forty-five in a black dress and a white apron, enters pushing a vacuum cleaner

Bethany Oh, I do beg your pardon, Hedwig. I didn't realize you were in here.

Hedwig (*who speaks with a German accent*) That's all right, Bethany. I've just come in from the garden. What a marvellous afternoon! I've been picking flowers and now I'm trying to arrange them artistically—and failing hopelessly, of course.

Bethany Well, I won't disturb you. I was going to go over this carpet before they all arrived, but it looks tidy enough, doesn't it?

Hedwig Immaculate. The most immaculate drawing-room in the county of Cumbria.

Bethany Well, it'll do.

Hedwig And what do you think of my flower arrangement? Come and give your expert opinion.

Bethany Oh, I've always loved that Waterford crystal vase.

Hedwig Well—do you approve?

Bethany (*horror-stricken as she sees the may blossom*) Hedwig! What on earth have you done?

Hedwig Ravishing, aren't they? The little treasures of the English hedgerows. Correction: the Lake District hedgerows. Why is everything up here twice as brightly coloured as everywhere else?

Bethany (*agitated*) Hedwig, my dear——

Hedwig Could it be the clouds bumping into the hills? The exceptional rainfall? But the richness of your landscape is shameful. Walt Disney would blush. William Wordsworth——

Bethany What have you done? Oh, suffering Sam! (*She snatches the may blossom from the vase*)

Hedwig Bethany! Mein Gott! What are you doing?

Bethany (*hurrying to the French windows*) No time—I'll tell you in a minute after I've got them out of the house.

Bethany runs into the garden

As Hedwig stares after her, the telephone rings. Hedwig lifts the receiver

Hedwig Gimmerbeck two-four-three . . . Yes, Patrick, darling . . . Oh, she just this minute *rushed* through the window with some flowers I picked . . . I don't know—some obscure old English custom, no doubt . . . The train arrived on time? . . . Ja, a very happy omen . . . Yes, I'll tell Bethany.

Bethany comes back

Yes, Patrick, darling. Drive carefully along those horrid lanes. Auf Wiedersehen. (*She replaces the receiver*)

Bethany Patrick?

Hedwig The train was on time and both passengers were safely on board.

Bethany I don't believe it.

Hedwig Tell me, why are the English so amazed when things run according to plan?

Bethany Just wait till you've been here a little longer, dear.

Hedwig I wonder why Patrick insisted on driving all the way to Oxenholme Station. Fifteen miles. They could easily have travelled on to Gimmerbeck Halt.

Bethany It would have meant too much messing about with luggage.

Hedwig And why did he go in that big floppy hat? He looked as though he was trying to disguise himself.

Bethany Did he?

Hedwig Yes—and that great conspiratorial cloak.

Bethany Oh, I suppose he wanted to make an artistic impression. You know Patrick. Now, Hedwig, this is vitally important. I want you to turn round three times.

Hedwig Turn round?

Bethany Yes, do a twirl. Quickly—there's no time to waste. Just as I do. (*Turning*) One! Two! Three!

Hedwig (*turning*) One! Two! Three! Is that all?

Bethany (*anxiously*) I can't think of anything else. Now listen, Hedwig, you must never bring may blossom into the house.

Hedwig What? That gorgeous pink—is that why you shot out like that?

Bethany Yes, that gorgeous pink may blossom off the hawthorn. Don't you have superstitions in Bavaria?

Hedwig Well, our grandfathers had superstitions and I suppose our less intelligent people have them still. In fact, Bavaria has some extremely bloodcurdling superstitions. What do may blossoms mean?

Bethany (*gravely*) Death.

Hedwig Death?

Bethany (*failing to make light of it*) A death in the house. Never mind, Hedwig, you couldn't be expected to know that. And perhaps there's a special dispensation for foreigners.

Hedwig (*Greta Garbo-ish*) I shall be the one.

Bethany I beg your pardon?

Hedwig If someone is to die . . . it must be me.

Bethany Nonsense, Hedwig.

Hedwig No. I am responsible. I must be the victim. A good German woman knows her duty.

Bethany But Hedwig——

Hedwig I shall take the only honourable path. Where does Patrick keep his shotgun?

Bethany Don't joke about it, Hedwig, whatever you do!

Hedwig Joke? When your life is at stake? And Patrick's? And Jack's. And the guests, who are at this very moment speeding in all innocence towards a house rendered deadly by my appalling ignorance of English custom and protocol and superstition? I say, those were three super nouns for a girl who spoke only pidgin English eight months ago: custom and protocol and superstition.

Bethany Yes, and you're picking up a very English sense of humour, too. But you mustn't joke about our superstitions. It can only make things worse.

Hedwig Bethany—a woman of your intelligence?

Bethany Imagination, Hedwig, not intelligence.

Hedwig There you are, you have an overdeveloped imagination. Lush and exaggerated, watered by these endless Lake District showers, twice as brighly coloured as other people's. And while we're on the subject of custom and protocol.

Bethany Yes?

Hedwig Before the guests arrive—I don't want to be stuffy—isn't that a divine adjective? I don't want to be stuffy, my dear, but don't you think that while guests are in the house we ought to drop this first-name thing?

Bethany (*hurt*) Do you think so?

Hedwig It's all splendid and democratic us being Hedwig and Bethany and Patrick to one another when we're alone, but don't you think . . . when we have guests? Or am I being frightfully Germanic and stuffy?

Bethany Well, if you really feel like that.

Hedwig I do, Bethany.

Bethany If it makes you more comfortable.

Hedwig Exactly. You don't mind, do you?

Bethany Well . . .

Hedwig I mean, I don't want to hurt your sensibilities through what you might take to be an excessive Germanic stuffiness.

Bethany Not at all.

Hedwig But when it comes down to brass farthings we do have a mistress and servant relationship, don't we?

Bethany (*coolly*) If you choose to see it that way. And by the way, the phrase is brass tacks.

Hedwig Oh, dear, I've trodden on your corners.

Bethany No no.

Hedwig I can see it in your eyes.

Bethany Not at all. You're quite right.

Hedwig Thank you, madam.

Bethany Just as long as you're happy, dear.

Hedwig Yes, madam. And you'd better give me your apron.

Bethany My apron?

Hedwig Madam, you look like the maid.

Bethany Oh.

Hedwig And I shall wear black.

Bethany I'd rather you didn't, Hedwig.

Hedwig But I look ravishing in black.

Bethany Then wear it by all means, but you mustn't expect to be ravished, even though Jack is coming home.

Hedwig I don't want any muddle with the guests, that's all. I want them to know where they stand. Where I stand. So they can order me to do things for them with a clear conscience—you follow? If you pass me off as a friend of the family——

Bethany But you are a friend of the family.

Hedwig Bethany—madam—I'm an au pair girl picking up the subtleties of the English tongue in your hospitable home. You're very sweet and considerate but life is much simpler if a person has a clearly-defined role and sticks to it. Even if it's a subservient role.

Bethany You are a funny girl.

Hedwig Not half as funny as you and Patrick, I assure you. Now—these guests. Patrick's been very mysterious about them.

Bethany Oh?

Hedwig And so have you, madam, so don't pretend innocence. I've caught you talking about them and suddenly stopping in the middle of the stream when I come into the room and looking conspiratorial and smug with each other.

Bethany (*a bit flustered*) Oh, dear. Well. You see, Patrick and I agreed we wouldn't say anything about it—about them—to you. But I don't see why not, honestly, now that it comes to the point.

Hedwig Good.

Bethany Only you must promise.

Hedwig I promise. I swear.

Bethany To play the game.

Hedwig A game? This gets better. What game?

Bethany Hedwig. Our friends . . . the guests . . . well . . .

Hedwig Yes?

Bethany Well, we've never met them before.

Hedwig Oh?

Bethany No, neither Patrick nor I have met them before. And now I really must get changed. They'll be here in a minute.

Hedwig One moment. What precisely do you mean?

Bethany No, I was afraid that wouldn't satisfy you. Must I go into it all? I suppose I must.

Hedwig Certainly you must.

Bethany Well, our guests . . .

Hedwig Yes?

Bethany Are our pen-friends. (*She gives an embarrassed laugh*)

Hedwig Pen-friends?

Bethany Yes. Patrick's and mine. There. Now I must go and change my dress.

Hedwig Let me understand. You mean you wrote letters to these people and they wrote letters to you?

Bethany How well you put it.

Hedwig From childhood?

Bethany Why, er, no.

Hedwig No? Then how long?

Bethany It's been going on for just over six months, yes.

Hedwig And our guests are a man and a woman, yes?

Bethany Why, er, yes.

Hedwig And the lady is your pen-friend and the man is Patrick's pen-friend?

Bethany Well, not abso- as you might say-lutely.

Hedwig You mean *you* have been in correspondence with an unknown man?

Bethany Yes.

Hedwig And Patrick has been in correspondence with an unknown woman?

Bethany Yes, and now I really must go and change. Oh, by the way, Patrick and I agreed that neither one of them must know the other is a pen-friend. We'll pass them off as old friends of ours.

Hedwig But have you and Patrick grown tired of one another?

Bethany Tired? Why?

Hedwig That you and he should look for new partners.

Bethany Oh, no, you've grasped quite the wrong end of the nettle. No, this isn't hanky-panky.

Hedwig No?

Bethany We saw this pen-friend column, you see, in this newspaper, quite by chance, and Patrick started reading them out, you see, just for a giggle actually, I'm sorry to say. But the more he read the more the giggles started to subside. It was extraordinary. The giggles just started to evaporate and in the end we sat there absolutely bereft . . . . of giggles. And we felt, well, we felt ashamed, because they were all such desperately lonely people, such sad—such broken lives, and they'd been driven to this as a last resort, and here were Patrick and I, who've been so lucky, laughing at their cries of distress.

Hedwig So you wrote to a man and he wrote to a woman.

Bethany What these people are longing for is a spot of friendly attention from the opposite sex.

Hedwig Isn't that playing with fireworks?

Bethany Oh, no, not if one keeps a sense of proportion. Not if you make it clear that your friendship is perfectly platonic. I mean, Ted knows I'm happily married.

Hedwig Ted?

Bethany He's named Ted Bithynian. Yes, and Patrick's forever praising my virtues to Kitty. Ted and Kitty can have no illusions on that score.

Hedwig Oh, poor Bethany, how little you know the human heart.

Bethany What do you mean?

Hedwig It always reads between the lines. Sometimes I think you're too innocent to be true.

Bethany What on earth do you mean?

Hedwig Sometimes you're a little too sweet. Like a cup of tea with too much sugar.

Bethany What a horrid thing to say. I've never been called a cup of tea before.

Hedwig Just take my warning. These people are coming here with expectations you can't fulfil.

Bethany Patrick was right. I should never have told you. Now you've got me terribly worried. The idea is for Ted to fall for Kitty, not for me.

Hedwig Oh, madam.

Bethany You don't think so?

Hedwig I'm certain. They are both lonely people, yes?

Bethany Yes.

Hedwig And why are lonely people lonely?

Bethany I couldn't start to answer that.

Hedwig Lonely people are lonely because they're so nasty that everybody avoids them.

Bethany How dreadfully cynical and heartless.

Hedwig Your Ted and Kitty have shown very clearly, by begging in public for a soulmate, that they're consumed by self-pity and egotism. They'll recognize themselves in each other straight away. They'll hate each other on sight.

Bethany Oh, Hedwig, they won't, will they?

Hedwig Show me their letters.

Bethany Why do you want to see their letters?

Hedwig So I can judge what kind of people they are.

Bethany I promised Patrick I wouldn't show those letters to a soul.

Hedwig There's an easy way round that. You can read them to me.

Bethany Wouldn't that be deceitful?

Hedwig Rubbish. Where are they. In the desk? In here? (*She goes to the* *desk, opens the top right-hand drawer, looks inside and finds a small blue-leather box)* In this little box, by any chance?

Bethany Hedwig! *(After a pause)* Oh, very well. But only one letter.

Hedwig One from each?

Bethany All right. Give them here.

Hedwig The introductory letter in each case, please.

Bethany All right, but not a word to Patrick, promise. Thank you. *(She sorts through the letters—some white, some violet-coloured)* I really ought to be changed by now. Now, the first letter from Ted . . . should be right on the bottom. Yes, here we are.

Hedwig The writing paper's a most disagreeable colour.

Bethany Violet? That's Kitty's. Now you said you wouldn't look.

Hedwig Sorry, I'll turn my back.

Bethany Well . . . the first one is dated . . . I can't quite make it out. I'm afraid poor Ted isn't very copperplate.

Hedwig Never mind the date. Proceed.

Bethany "Dear Mrs Silverlock, Many thanks for your kind and understanding letter and the pot of delicious home-made strawberry jam. In you I recognize that rare animal a woman of compassion."

Hedwig Ah-ha!

Bethany "I note that you are happily married and can only say long may it flourish. Also you are blessed with a healthy young son of twenty-two away at agricultural college. Congrats again." Did I hear a car?

Hedwig No. Go on.

Bethany "I myself was a teenage bridegroom but it soon developed that we were two trains running on the same track in different directions and it didn't last. I find as we loners all do that the evenings are full of solitude, but I have an affectionate cat and my job as a salesman of textured wall-coatings helps to dim the despair. My interests are legion and include do-it-yourself, light classics, birds, flowers and anything to do with farms. Although never bored, a lot is missing from my life. Your handwriting is cultivated and genteel, so perhaps we could establish a rapport. Do you agree with me that decency, proportion and sensitivity are rated low in today's market? Ted"—he's signing off now —"Ted from the land of the highlands and lowlands, has made his plea. Dare I hope?" And that's it.

Hedwig Dare he hope? What does he mean by that?

The telephone rings and Hedwig answers it

Gimmerbeck two-four-three . . . I'm sorry, he's out at the moment . . . Would you like to speak to Mrs Silverlock? . . . Bill? . . . I beg your pardon? Did you say old Bill? . . . Roll out the red carpet? . . . What invitation? . . . Wait, I don't understand. Oh, he's gone. *(She hangs up)*

Bethany Who was it?

Hedwig Somebody named Bill. Do you know him?

Bethany Bill?

Hedwig A friend of Patrick's. He said he might be delayed.

Bethany Delayed doing what?

Hedwig Coming here. He said he was coming to take up Patrick's long-standing invitation and we must roll out a red carpet.

Bethany He can't. We've got a full house. Bill who? What invitation?

Hedwig I've no idea. He said he'll ring again. Patrick can put him off.

Bethany Yes, but I don't know any Bill.

Hedwig Never mind Bill. Read me Kitty's letter.

Bethany I'm not changed yet.

Hedwig You promised.

Bethany Oh, dear, very well. Kitty. Now—here we are. "Dear Mr Silver-lock"——

Hedwig That paper's an awful colour.

Bethany "Dear Mr Silverlock, It was a very real thrill to get your beautiful letter and pot of jam and to think there is still a little kindness left in the world. How wonderful that a professional artist can find the time to write to little me. I hope your good wife is keeping well and does not object to your writing. Since losing my husband a few years back I've also lost my interest in life, but now I'm ready to spread my wings. What I look for in a man is gentleness and courtesy. I have no objection to anybody drinking and smoking in moderation"—Hedwig! There's somebody coming in through the garden. Oh, these letters!

In their eagerness to put the letters away, Bethany and Hedwig manage to drop them all over the floor. They get down on their knees and start to gather them up

> *Patrick, aged fifty, enters through the french windows, followed by Ted, aged thirty-five, and Kitty, a very attractive red-head aged thirty*

Patrick Well, here we are, and about time too!

Bethany Oh, Patrick!

Patrick Come on, come on, you two. Don't be shy. Thought I'd bring them in through the garden.

Bethany (*on her knees*) Oh, that's nice, darling. Why don't you show them the auriculas?

Patrick Yes, here we are, this is Kitty and this is Ted. But what am I talking about? One would think you'd never met them before. Ha-ha! (*After a pause*) What on earth are you two doing on your hands and knees?

Bethany I was just tidying up these letters.

Patrick Letters? Oh, those.

Ted Let me give you a hand, Mrs—ah—Bethany.

Bethany No, no, Ted, we'll manage.

Kitty Yes, many hands make light work. Let me help. Oh, that pretty violet paper.

Bethany Yes, it is, isn't it? Please don't bother. I think we've got them all now. There.

Hedwig Yes, I'll put them in the desk.

Ted Well, Bethany, I must say you're looking fitter and lovelier than ever. What about a little kiss? *He kisses Hedwig*

Hedwig Thank you, but I'm Hedwig.
Ted Hedwig?
Hedwig The au pair.
Patrick Just Ted's little joke. Ha-ha! Still the great leg-puller, Ted, eh?
   Ha-ha.
Ted What? Oh, yes. Hullo, Bethany. Fantastic to meet you.
Patrick Again.
Ted Eh? Oh, yes, sure, again. Fantastic to meet you again.
Bethany Welcome to Gimmerbeck, Ted.
Patrick Again.
Bethany Again, yes, of course. And Kitty dear, welcome to Gimmerbeck—
   again.
Kitty It's so very nice to meet you at last, Bethany.

Pause

Kitty   ⎫
Bethany ⎬ *(together)* Again. *(They all laugh)*
Patrick   ⎭
Bethany Did you both have good journeys?
Ted A dream. All the way from Scotland.
Kitty Marvellous. Perfect connections all the way from Liverpool.
Bethany Splendid. I must say, Ted, you're much younger than I——
Patrick Than he was the last time we saw him, yes.
Bethany Much. And *you*, Kitty. Such lovely red hair.
Patrick As always. Ha-ha.
Bethany Of course, you've always had the most gorgeous red hair, Kitty,
   haven't you?
Patrick Look, I think you two had better go and look at your rooms and
   wash off the travel stains and so forth, eh?
Bethany Oh, yes, I'll show you where you are.
Patrick No, no, let Hedwig do that, my dear. All right, Hedwig, show Mr
   and Mrs—ah—Kitty and Ted——
Hedwig Yes, sir. This way, please.
Ted Yes, right.
Hedwig Watch the vacuum cleaner. I'd better take it out.
Ted Can I give you a hand?
Hedwig I'll manage, sir.

   Hedwig goes out taking the vacuum cleaner

Ted and Kitty go to the door

Kitty See you soon, then.
Patrick Jump in the bath if you like.
Bethany Or the shower. There's oodles of hot water.
Patrick Then come down and join us in a noggin.
Ted *(laughing)* I might just do that.

   Kitty leaves, followed by Ted

Patrick Well, that went fairly smoothly.

Bethany Yes.
Patrick Except for the letters.
Bethany I'm sorry, Patrick.
Patrick Refreshing your memory?
Bethany I'm sorry. Hedwig twisted my arm.
Patrick Hedwig?
Bethany I told her the full story.
Patrick Why on earth did you do that?
Bethany Oh, you know how she gets round one.
Patrick And you let her read the letters?
Bethany Just enough to put her in the picture.
Patrick I turn my back for ten minutes and you spill the beans.
Bethany I don't see what harm it can do.
Patrick Wasn't she suspicious?
Bethany Oh, you know Hedwig. She just thought we were a bit dotty,
that's all.
Patrick Are you sure?
Bethany Don't worry, darling, we'll soon be disposing of Hedwig.
Patrick Yes. Pity that. Pity.
Bethany Unless of course you'd like to keep her. She's very decorative
about the place.
Patrick The trouble is we couldn't afford it.

The telephone rings

I'll get it. (*He answers the telephone*) Hello, Patrick Silverlock speaking. . . . Old Bill? . . . I'm awfully sorry. . . . Oh, really? Over a cattlegrid? . . . Yes, yes, damned nuisance, but listen, old man, are you sure
it's me you want to speak to? . . . What invitation was that then? . . .
Bill who? . . . What do you mean: I'll know you when I see you? . . .
Hello? We haven't got a red carpet. Hello? Hello, hello? . . . Gone.
(*He replaces the receiver*) Blasted queer.

Bethany I take it that was Bill.
Patrick Oh, he's a friend of yours, is he?
Bethany No, he just rang earlier. Hedwig spoke to him. She couldn't make
top or tail of him.
Patrick Neither could I. Said I'd invited him here.
Bethany Do you think he was sober?
Patrick Said he'd got a puncture going over a cattlegrid. Do you think he
was drunk?
Bethany He doesn't sound very coherent.
Patrick Could it be some pal of Jack's?
Bethany Jack wouldn't invite somebody without telling us.
Patrick Jack not here yet?
Bethany He said about six.
Patrick I just don't know any Bill, d'you see?
Bethany I shouldn't worry. We can always turn him from the door.
Patrick That's true.
Bethany Ted and Kitty seem very sweet.

Patrick Awfully, yes.
Bethany But much younger than I'd imagined.
Patrick So I noticed.
Bethany Much. Doesn't it strike you as odd?
Patrick What?
Bethany That two such attractive people——
Patrick She really is a cracker, all that lovely flame-coloured hair.
Bethany That two such beautiful and sweet young people should have to
    look for pen-friends?
Patrick They're shy, there's the rub. There are thousands like that; nice
    people, lovely people, perfectly happy on the outside but without the
    confidence to establish relationships. Confidence shattered by something
    in the past. The big cities are full of them.
Bethany And to think that not a living soul would miss them if anything
    happened.
Patrick That's the world for you in nineteen eighty-two.
Bethany Do you think they took a fancy to each other?
Patrick They were terribly shy with each other. Avoiding each other's
    eyes. Hardly exchanged a word. But I think I detected something . . .
    flashing between them. Signals going to and fro.
Bethany I do hope it comes off.
Patrick Don't worry, it's all under control.
Bethany It's just that something a bit shocking happened while you were
    out.
Patrick Oh?
Bethany Yes, Hedwig brought some may blossom into the house. You
    know what that means.
Patrick How very prophetic.
Bethany Well, it gave me quite a shock.
Patrick May blossom! (*He laughs*)

Ted comes in wearing more casual dress

Ted Well, all spruced up now.
Bethany Oh, Ted. Did you find everything?
Ted Yes, thank you. Beautiful. Grand. It's a fantastic room. Those bars
    at the window——
Patrick Yes, talking of bars, what would you like to drink?

Kitty comes in wearing a stunning dress

Bethany Kitty, what a lovely dress! Doesn't Kitty look ravishing, Ted?

No answer

    Ted?
Ted Sorry. I was miles away.
Bethany I said isn't Kitty beautiful?
Ted (*looking at Kitty as if for the first time*) Oh. Yes. I suppose so.
Kitty Perhaps I'm not his type. I'm afraid he isn't mine.

Bethany Oh.

Ted No, Kitty isn't my type. Nothing personal, mind you. I go for the more mature woman, that's all.

Kitty How strange. I go for the more mature man.

Bethany Well, first appearances often fool us. I couldn't stand the sight of Patrick when we met, could I, darling?

Patrick Good Lord, couldn't you? Kitty, a sherry?

Kitty Something longer if you have it. I'm as dry as old bones.

Patrick Lager, lemonade?

Kitty Super, yes, lemonade.

Patrick Ted?

Ted A sherry would be fantastic at this point in time.

Bethany Drink-wise.

Patrick How about you, Bethany?

Bethany Oh, not for me. I've got to go up and change. It'll give you two young people the chance to get acquainted.

Patrick goes to the drinks cabinet and pours the drinks

And I think you'd better come along, too, Patrick. I want you to tenderize the steak.

Patrick Oh, I was going to join them in a little drink.

Bethany So that Ted and Kitty will have a chance to get acquainted.

Patrick Ah, yes, beat up the old beefsteak. There you are, Kitty. (*He hands her a drink*)

Kitty Thank you, Patrick.

Patrick (*handing Ted a drink*) Ted?

Ted Oh, thanks. Cheers.

Bethany Come on, Patrick. Bring that with you. (*She indicates his drink*)

Patrick Oh, right you are. Well, ah, see you later. You two get . . . acquainted.

Bethany If you want a topper-up, you know where it is. Come on, Patrick.

Patrick Yes. Don't be shy, you two. Circulate.

Bethany and Patrick go out

Ted (*after a pause*) Well, cheers. Kitty.

Kitty Happy times. Ted.

Ted Lovely old couple.

Kitty Not all that old.

Ted No, no, I didn't mean that. Known them long?

Kitty Oh, for some time.

Ted Yes, same here.

Kitty Beautiful outlook.

Ted Fantastic. A bit isolated.

Kitty Fantastic.

Ted Would you say those were the Langdale Pikes?

Kitty I'm not very well up on pikes.

Pause

Ted ⎱
Kitty ⎰ (*together*) Do you come here often?

Ted Sorry. After you.

Kitty Do you come here often?

Ted Only in the mug-hunting season.

Kitty How peculiar. So do I.

Ted Can I top you up?

Kitty Thank you.

Ted (*pouring two more drinks*) How are things back home?

Kitty I planted the potatoes.

Ted I should hope so. Here you are.

Kitty Thanks. I was as dry as old bones. I had the decorators in. Pompadour pink and stark white. I got a new bottle of scent. It's called "Sexpot".

Ted Fantastic.

Kitty I'm not wearing it now. This is called "Tease".

Ted (*after a pause*) How about a kiss?

Kitty What if somebody walks in?

Ted We could say we were an old married couple.

Kitty How did you get on in Scotland?

Ted It was a very posh set-up. You know—crystal chandeliers and gold chairs. I came away with nine thousand pounds and a silver fish-set.

Kitty Yes, you told me in your letter. I mean the wife.

Ted Oh, so-so. A few cuts above this one, but then she was young, wasn't she? Hardly been used. One previous owner. Very little on the clock. (*He laughs*) Good heavens, you are, aren't you?

Kitty What?

Ted After all this time—jealous.

Kitty Aren't you?

Ted Sweetheart, it's just a clinical transaction. How many times have I told you? Feelings don't come into it.

Kitty The husband in Southampton was an absolute dish.

Ted How nice for you.

Kitty You don't care, do you?

Ted Yes I do. How much did you take him for?

Kitty Fifteen thousand. What if I'd fallen in love with him?

Ted You'd have played fair with me.

Kitty What do you mean?

Ted You'd have given me my seven and a half.

Kitty And that's all you're worried about?

Ted I'm not worried because I'm sure of you.

Kitty I wish I could be sure of you.

Ted We've had this out a hundred times. It's just a job of work.

Kitty Yes, but you seem to enjoy it so much.

Ted You object to me enjoying my work?

Kitty Yes, this work.

Ted Well, we can give it a rest for a while after this job. This is the big one. We might even be able to retire.

Kitty My God, I hope so. It's wearing me out. And we could give Sally a bit more attention.

Ted Is she still sucking her thumb?

Kitty It's making her all bucktoothed. Listen, Ted, are you sure this is all such a pure coincidence?

Ted What?

Kitty Patrick writing to me and Bethany writing to you.

Ted Look, on the law of averages it was bound to happen sooner or later. I mean, six years.

Kitty I don't think there is any law of averages, is there?

Ted All right, there is no law of averages, but for six years we've been pushing out our cunningly-worded little appeals. Six years. Newspapers, magazines, Julie Dawn. God bless Julie Dawn. Thousands of replies flowing back. Thousands of soft-centred mugs. Each one unintentionally laying bare a huge hole in his or her emotional make-up, dreaming that we'll fill it, laying themselves wide open to all kinds of skulduggery, did they but know it.

Kitty Yes, but a husband and wife.

Ted So one day a husband and wife see the same agony column. They take the same paper, don't they? There we are in the same agony column —your touching plea, my touching plea. God bless the agony column. Ten to one they start off by having a laugh. "I say, my dear, this is awfully amusing, what?" Then suddenly something happens. They start feeling sorry. It's not funny when you boil it all down. Between those stilted lines, those naïve inarticulate phrases, they start to make out dimly something that—they start to read the heartbreak. Bang and we're in.

Kitty Yes, I know all that.

Ted And the beauty of it is that they're deceiving themselves. Compassion my foot. It's not compassion that makes them rush to put pen to paper. It's boredom.

Kitty Yes, I know all that, Ted.

Ted By responding to an appeal like that they're uttering a great shout for help. "My marriage has gone stale! Let me out!" They're ready for an adventure. And once they've had it they start to panic.

Kitty I know all that. Ted. I've read *Psychology for Profit* as well. Three times.

Ted *Psychology for Profit.* Professor Fred H. Pye. The book that changed our lives. Do you realize? If it wasn't for Fred H. Pye we'd still be leaping in and out of french windows in weekly rep.

Kitty I grant you that, but I still feel a bit edgy about this set-up.

Ted First night butterflies, that's all.

Kitty No, it's not just that. There was something that happened on the way here.

Ted Oh?

Kitty In the car. It was just that—no. You'll only laugh at me.

Ted No, go on. I won't laugh.

Kitty Well, as we were driving along—no, I know you'll laugh at me.

Ted Laugh? I've said I won't, haven't I? Hell's teeth.

Kitty Well, it was . . . I saw a magpie.

Ted You saw a magpie?

Kitty One magpie.

Ted (*laughing*) Is that all? She saw one magpie!

Kitty You promised you wouldn't.

Ted Yes, but I ask you . . .

Kitty One magpie. One for sorrow, two for joy, three for a letter, four for a boy. And I saw just one. One for sorrow.

Ted (*laughing*) That's just an idiotic superstition.

Kitty I knew you'd laugh at me.

Ted Anyway, isn't there something you can do about a magpie? Salute it or something? Then it won't harm you?

Kitty I did salute it.

Ted Well, you're all right then.

Kitty How do I know it *saw* me salute?

Ted Why? Didn't it salute back? Good heavens, Kitty, stop going on about magpies. We've got a job to do. Think of Sally's future.

Kitty Sorry.

Ted So the question is—tactics.

Kitty Right.

Ted Softly softly or smash and grab?

Kitty Hard to get or frontal attack with all guns blazing?

Ted In my experience, the trouble with playing hard to get is that some people are just too lazy to make the effort.

Kitty Yes, and if they're the nervous type a frontal attack can scare them silly.

Ted You know, it isn't an easy life.

Kitty We earn our money.

Ted Have you sized this pair up yet?

Kitty Patrick and Bethany? Well, they strike me as being rather nervy about the whole thing—like a nicely brought-up girl on her first date.

Ted Right, right. Rather shy and reserved but bursting to be kissed. Yes, that's how I read it.

Kitty I don't think they're going to make the first move.

Ted No, I think you're right. So it looks like rush tactics.

Kitty Sweep them off their feet.

Ted Right, right. Thank God I've kept my looks.

Kitty There's only one thing troubling me, Ted.

Ted Yes?

Kitty You don't think Patrick and Bethany could be playing some game of their own, do you?

Ted What a nasty twisted mind you've got.

Kitty You twisted it.

Ted And who lives like a Duchess? Which address did you use?

Kitty Wallasey. You?

Ted Dunbarton.

Kitty It's going to be charming under one roof. You seducing another woman and me seducing another man.

Ted Just don't take it personally.

Kitty I'm just agog to see your technique, that's all.

Ted Come here and I'll show you.

Kitty Technique? No, thanks.

Ted Come here.

Kitty Just to keep your hand in?

Ted I haven't seen you for five weeks. To hell with technique. (*He takes her in his arms*)

Kitty I can't be sure of you any more. That's the trouble with marrying a professional charmer.

Ted Listen, I love you.

Kitty Ha!

Ted Kitty, I love you to despair.

Kitty How prettily it rolls off the tongue, but you've had such a lot of practice.

Ted What can I say? Listen, my lovely precious darling.

Kitty Words.

Ted I could never leave off loving you, Kitty, damn you.

Kitty But how can I believe it?

Ted Listen, Kitty, this beautiful body——

Kitty Let go of me, Ted.

Ted This body belongs to me, these lovely high cheekbones, and these green eyes, and this fantastic blazing hair.

Kitty Ted! Be careful!

Ted All of you belongs to me—understand? Every inch.

Kitty I believe you!

Ted And I worship every fragment. Every freckle.

Kitty Ted! Not here!

Ted Every atom.

Kitty We've only just met! Let me go!

Ted And I want to sink my teeth into those lovely snowy biceps.

Kitty Not now, Ted.

Ted And crush those soft—those plump and juicy lips. Crush them!

Kitty Ted! Stop it! Oh! Aah! Darling! Ooooh!

Ted (*bending her backwards in a passionate kiss*) Aah, Kitty!

The door opens and Hedwig comes in

Hedwig Mein Gott!

Ted and Kitty turn to look at her

Sorry! I see you've become acquainted.

CURTAIN

SCENE 2

The same. 7 p.m. that evening

As the CURTAIN *rises the room is deserted*

Ted comes in through the door, wearing a dinner jacket

Ted (*brightly*) Hello? Anybody about?

*When it is plain nobody is, his attitude changes to one of businesslike brisk-
ness. He goes to the french windows and stares out, then returns to the door,
which he opens and closes to ensure he won't be disturbed. He goes to the
desk and makes an expert rapid search of the drawers, pausing once to read
a typewritten document. Then he goes about the room picking up and
examining objects that might be of value, for instance taking a small painting
from the wall to look for authentication and upturning china ornaments
to read ceramic marks. He takes one of a pair of candlesticks from the
fireplace, puts a jeweller's glass in his eye, studies the hallmark and whistles
in admiration. As he is returning the candlestick to its place the door opens*

*Bethany enters and Ted whips round to gaze at her sternly. She is dressed
attractively for dinner*

(*Stern and tense*) Bethany—don't move—just stand there.

Bethany Ted——

Ted No—don't say anything. I just want to drink you in. (*He pauses as
he drinks her in*) Bethany—you look stunning.

Bethany (*girlishly delighted*) Oh, Ted, you glib-tongued flatterer you. You
look rather distinguished yourself. (*She advances into the room*) But you
poor boy, have they left you all alone?

Ted Patrick said he'd show Kitty the early-flowering heathers before dinner.

Bethany Well, they should have taken you with them.

Ted Oh, they offered. I wanted to wait for you. I didn't want to see it
without you. I think of it as one of our—enchanted places.

Bethany (*uneasily*) Oh? Oh, really.

Ted You've told me so much about it. The azaleas and the lilac. The
honeysuckle. I've often pictured us, at dusk, among the early-flowering
heathers. Spicy scents of evening. The swallows and martins dipping
and gliding.

Bethany And to think you've got no garden of your own. It makes me feel
quite guilty. Do you go in for window boxes?

Ted In Dunbarton?

Bethany Not a gardeney place?

Ted My window won't even open. It's one of those big sash windows and
at some point in its history it's got twisted and jammed in the frame. I've
tried everything. My landlord won't spend a penny.

Bethany I really do feel awful, having so much. And you live in just the
one room?

Ted Me and the Baby Belling. The single bed in the right-hand corner.
The built-in sink and the built-in wardrobe. The all-purpose drop-leaf
table and the massive fumed-oak chest of drawers.

Bethany I can see it, Ted, all too starkly.

Ted The sagging armchair in front of the two-bar electric fire.

Bethany Dunbarton. Aren't there any presentable young ladies in Dunbarton?

Ted In Dunbarton?

Bethany No, I see.

Ted Do you subscribe . . . Bethany, do you tag along with the idea that there's an infinite choice for a man looking for a mate?

Bethany I'm sorry?

Ted Or for a woman looking for a man? What I'm driving at—some people hold that there are any number of women a man would be happy with, that the world's littered with them.

Bethany Oh, yes, I see what you mean.

Ted I think there's just one woman. Just one spot-on partner. And the chances of finding her?

Bethany Not good?

Ted It needs a miracle.

Bethany Yes, I can see that.

Ted I know I'm an old-fashioned romantic, but when I got your letter——

Bethany What do you think of Kitty?

Ted Who?

Bethany Kitty.

Ted Er, Kitty?

Bethany You know. Kitty?

Ted Oh, Kitty. Yes.

Bethany Don't you find her rather—well—isn't she quite outstandingly beautiful?

Ted Kitty?

Bethany That absolute abundance of silky red hair?

Ted Oh, there are stacks of girls with good looks. The streets of Dunbarton are full of them.

Bethany Like Kitty?

Ted Droves of them. But what they haven't got is the insight of sympathy. Depth. Something that arouses a sort of instinctive ache. When I got your first letter, Bethany——

Bethany I'm so glad you liked the jam.

Ted That fantastic jam! Hell's teeth, how do you make it?

Bethany Well, it's quite simple, really. You need lots of sugar and then there's the fruit of course—but good heavens, you don't want to be bored with jam recipes.

Ted No, honestly, it's fascinating.

Bethany Going on just like one of my silly letters.

Ted Silly? Listen, your letters are beautiful. Did you ever think of taking up writing?

Bethany With all their chatter about the Women's Institute and blackfly in the beans and shopping expeditions into Keswick and Jack's exam results?

Ted No, don't you see? It's what you make of the minutiae of country life, the humour that bubbles through, the warmth, the sort of overwhelming tenderness.

Bethany Oh, come, Ted.

Ted No, I mean it. I think you could be another Jane Austen. Have you ever tried? Have you ever sat down seriously and written a story?

Bethany Well, I did, once, as a matter of fact.

Ted I knew. I knew.

Bethany It was a competition organized by the WI.

Ted Well.

Bethany I won second prize.

Ted Too subtle for them.

Bethany A big jar of pickled walnuts.

Ted See? Your first attempt. I'd love to see it. Have you still got it?

Bethany Oh, we've eaten it all long since. Patrick's terribly fond of pickled walnuts.

Ted I don't think he appreciates you, does he?

Bethany Patrick?

Ted It comes over in your letters.

Bethany Oh, surely not.

Ted And when I saw you together, it was there.

Bethany What was there?

Ted Taking you for granted. He was a bit abrupt with you.

Bethany Abrupt? When?

Ted And letting you go about dressed as the maid. That speaks for itself.

Bethany My black dress?

Ted That's how he regards you. I should say he wasn't the world's most sensitive man, am I right?

Bethany Patrick's got a very loving heart.

Ted But have you ever asked yourself—and I think you have, because you're a bit of a brooder, aren't you?—have you ever asked yourself if he's the one?

Bethany I'm sorry, Ted, I'm not quite with you.

Ted The One.

Bethany The one?

Ted The one spot-on dovetailed partner you had that astronomically slender chance of finding.

Bethany Well . . .

Ted Be truthful.

Bethany Well . . .

Ted Be honest with yourself.

Bethany Well, we rub along together perfectly adequately.

Ted Ah, but that's not enough for you, Bethany.

Bethany No?

Ted Look, people put up with second best but they're afraid to admit it. We're conditioned to it, a remarkably docile species, adaptable, make do and don't grumble. But we have inner voices, talking to us all the time, they come out at night, two in the morning. "Are you really content?" they say. "Is this all? Couldn't I find something better?" And they make us feel guilty. Guilty because that's the way we've been conditioned, how society's moulded us into suppressing our innermost longings. Brush them under the carpet, get on with your humdrum existence, or else. What do you do, Bethany? Two in the morning and you can't sleep?

Bethany Patrick goes down and gets me a glass of milk and an aspirin and I drop off like a light.

Ted Don't you think I couldn't read your hidden messages?

Bethany Hidden messages?

Ted Who knows, they might even be hidden from you, bouncing around your subconscious mind.

Bethany Well no, by definition I wouldn't be conscious of those.

Ted But they cry out!

Bethany Hidden messages?

Ted Leaping out from every page you write.

Bethany To Dunbarton?

Ted Bethany, don't let's pretend.

Bethany Pretend?

She backs away but he follows

Ted You're the one.

Bethany The one?

Ted Out of all the hopeless billions.

Bethany Me? For you, you mean?

Ted Bethany, I love you to despair. (*He takes her by the arms*)

Bethany No, Ted, I won't have you talking like that.

He tries to kiss her

   Ted! Please let go of me.

Ted Listen, my lovely precious darling.

Bethany Ted, if Patrick were to come in!

Ted Let him find out the truth.

Bethany You're hurting me.

Ted Don't you see? It's not Patrick you belong to. This beautiful body belongs to me, those delicate cheekbones, those grey eyes flecked with gold, this fantastic brown hair.

Bethany Ted! You must let go of me.

Ted All of you belongs to me. Every inch. And I worship every fragment. Every atom.

Bethany Ted!

Ted I want to sink my teeth in those lovely creamy shoulders.

Bethany Ted!

Ted And crush those soft juicy lips. (*He kisses her*)

Bethany Ted! Don't! Oh! Aaah.

Ted My precious wonderful love. (*He bends her backwards in a passionate kiss*)

The door opens and Hedwig comes in wearing a maid's uniform

Hedwig Mein Gott! So sorry! I'll go.

Bethany Hedwig——

Hedwig Auf Wiedersehen.

Hedwig goes out and closes the door

Ted Does that girl never knock?

Bethany Before today there was never any reason why she should. What on earth is she going to think? I must go and have a word with her—explain——

Ted Tell her I was getting a fly out of your eye. Come on, I'll back you up.

Bethany A fly? Oh, that's terribly lame.

Ted Give your eye a rub. Make it red.

Bethany Is that all right?

Ted Fantastic. Come on.

He leads her out

Patrick and Kitty come in through the french windows. She carries a bunch of flowers

Patrick (*as he enters*) Hello? Anybody there? Funny. Nobody here, Kitty. Must be getting togged up for dinner.

Kitty Where shall I put these flowers?

Patrick Oh there's that vase . . . here. I'll get some water. Hello, we're in luck. Water in it.

Kitty Lesser spotted orchids. I didn't think such things grew in England.

Patrick Can't keep 'em down. (*He hands her the vase*)

Kitty Oh, what are these little pink petals floating in this water?

Patrick Let me see. Oh, those, just blossom or something.

Kitty Patrick, I do believe it's may blossom. Somebody's had may blossom in this vase.

Patrick Really?

Kitty But that's terrible.

Patrick Eh?

Kitty Yes, didn't you know? (*She heads for the french windows*) I'm going to empty it in the garden.

Patrick Oh, right, empty away.

Kitty is away a few seconds and then returns

Kitty (*returning*) I watered one of your geraniums.

Patrick Thank you.

Kitty I don't know if this vase should be sterilized or what.

Patrick Oh?

Kitty May blossom shouldn't come into the house. It brings death.

Patrick Death? Does it really? Imagine that now.

Kitty Yes, you'll have to change something over to placate the—er—demonic influences.

Patrick Change something over?

Kitty Yes, to change the bad luck.

Patrick Ah, yes, to propitiate the . . . Anything you say, dear girl. What do you suggest? Look, shall I change these candlesticks over on the mantelpiece?

Kitty Oh, no, it has to be something you're wearing.

Patrick (*at a loss, looking down at his clothes*) Ah . . . well.

Kitty Your socks would do.

Patrick My socks? Right, splendid, nothing simpler. (*He sits down and removes his shoes and socks*) Socks it is. Now there—one sock. Do excuse this rather beastly-looking old foot of mine.

Kitty It's a very handsome foot.

Patrick Do you think so?

Kitty Really rather distinguished-looking.

Patrick Now—that's the other. Toe-nails need cutting. (*He wiggles his toes for a moment, then puts his socks and shoes back on*) Right, there we are. Fine. That's the evil eye warded off for another day.

Kitty Yes, you're safe now.

Patrick That's a relief. How about a drink to celebrate?

Kitty I'm still at risk.

Patrick Oh?

Kitty Yes, I've got to change something over as well.

Patrick Oh.

Kitty Or I'm in mortal peril.

Patrick (*gesturing helplessly at her clothes*) Well—couldn't you—no . . .

Kitty I've got nothing on, really, that I—except my blouse.

Patrick Yes—I mean no. Wouldn't your shoes . . .?

Kitty Shoes?

Patrick No.

Kitty It'll have to be the blouse.

Patrick (*uneasily*) Ah.

Kitty I'll put it on back to front. It shouldn't look too bad. (*She starts undoing the buttons at the front*)

Patrick (*alarmed*) Wouldn't you like to pop upstairs?

Kitty No, it'll only take a second. Just these three buttons.

Patrick Look—I'll run along and tell Bethany we're back.

Kitty There. It's off.

Patrick I'll just run along and tell Bethany——

Kitty No, no, Patrick. I want you.

Patrick What?

Kitty Come here, you silly boy. I won't eat you. I just want you to do the buttons up at the back.

Patrick Yes, well, I should slip it on quickly. Don't want you catching a chill.

The door opens and Ted comes in

Ted Hello, you two. Oh.

Patrick (*startled*) Ah, Ted.

Ted It's all right. Don't mind me. Carry on. I'm only passing through.

Patrick We were just—er—warding off the evil eye.

Ted Oh, is that how you do it? Fantastic. Don't mind me. Just on my way out to the garden. Bethany wants me to cut a sprig of rosemary.

Patrick Oh, yes, straight past the brassicas.

Ted Beg pardon?

Patrick Straight past the cabbages.

Ted Oh, yes, brassicas. Right. (*He goes to the french windows*) Sorry to butt in. I won't come back this way. Leave you two alone.
Patrick No, that's all right, Ted.
Ted I can see when I'm in the way. One hint's enough to a wise man.

Ted goes out into the garden

Patrick (*staring after him*) Now what did he mean by that? Do put it on, Kitty.
Kitty I'm sure he's seen more in his time. (*She puts her blouse on*) There—will you do these buttons for me?
Patrick (*fiddling with the buttons behind her*) Yes, there we are. That's got one of them. Would you mind keeping still?
Kitty Do you like my scent?
Patrick There—all buttoned up and shipshape.

Kitty turns and stands quite close to him

Kitty It's called "Tease".
Patrick Oh, really? You mean as in cream teas?
Kitty (*laughing*) No, dear, never mind.
Patrick Do you think we're immune now?
Kitty Immune?
Patrick From the evil doo-das and so forth.
Kitty Oh, yes, I should think we've exorcized them all away. Do you think I'm foolish—believing in these superstitions?
Patrick Not at all.
Kitty Most men would.
Patrick Oh?
Kitty Yes, they haven't the imagination.
Patrick Ah.
Kitty You're a very understanding man, Patrick, if I may say so.
Patrick (*modestly*) Oh, no, no.
Kitty I knew it even before I saw you.
Patrick Really?
Kitty Those letters. They were permeated with it. Did you ever think of taking up writing?
Patrick What? Those dreadful screeds?
Kitty Dreadful? They saved my life. They restored my faith in the wise and warm human spirit. I know that sounds pretentious, but that's what they did. There was such solid wisdom in them.
Patrick Wait a minute. Are you sure you're not mixing me up with somebody else?
Kitty No! I'm talking about you! Your letters. They had—a certain profundity—and at the same time a humanity. An undercurrent of gaiety—and yet a steady serene philosophy.
Patrick Which letter in particular are you referring to?
Kitty Oh, all of them, all of them!
Patrick That I wrote to you?
Kitty Yes—yes!

Patrick I thought they were mostly about pottering about in the garden.

Kitty They were about Life. They were about Living. (*She pauses, and casually looks at her leg*) Oh, look, I've got a run in my tights.

Patrick What?

Kitty I must have caught it on the roses. Look.

Patrick (*increasingly embarrassed*) Yes, they need cutting back.

Kitty (*lifting her skirt*) You see? Just below the knee.

Patrick (*looking elsewhere*) Why, so it is.

Kitty Gracious, it goes on and on . . . look . . . and on.

Patrick Care for a drink, would you?

Kitty Up and up.

Patrick Er, I should put your dress down, Kitty.

Kitty Look at that, right on, up and up.

Patrick Lager, lemonade, Martini?

Kitty Look, it goes right to the top of my leg. Where are you going, Patrick?

Patrick What? Looking for my pipe.

Kitty You can't be embarrassed.

Patrick Oh, in my pocket all the time.

Kitty Patrick, I don't mind. You can look at my legs.

Patrick Matches. Have you seen my matches?

Kitty After all, they do belong to you.

Patrick Eh? Oh, here they are all the time. In the other pocket. (*He starts filling a pipe nervously*)

Kitty I said my legs belong to you. All of me belongs to you. Don't pretend you don't know, Patrick.

Patrick I'm sorry? What?

Kitty Don't start lighting your pipe. Not now.

Patrick No?

Kitty Look at my legs, Patrick.

Patrick (*dropping the matches*) Oh, dash it! Look at that. Matches all over the carpet.

Kitty Let them lie there. Didn't you feel it in the garden?

Patrick Feel it? (*He goes down on his knees to gather matches*)

Kitty That I belong to you. That you belong to me.

Patrick I'd better clear these matches up. No, no—no need for you to get down on your hands and knees.

But Kitty joins him all the same

Kitty (*laughing*) Why not?

Patrick Please stand up. I can manage very well.

Kitty Patrick, you've got to look the truth in the eye.

Patrick (*panicky laughter*) What a scene!

Kitty What are you laughing at?

Patrick If somebody should come in, that's all. Us crawling about on the carpet.

Kitty I know you're going to make your move some time during the weekend. Why not own up to it?

Patrick Oh, look, there's one! Trying to hide behind the leg of that chair.

Kitty Patrick! (*She grabs his ankle*)

Patrick I say, that hurts. Please let go of my ankle, Kitty.

Kitty Turn round and look me in the eye.

Patrick I'd be much happier if you stood up and let me get on with collecting these matches.

Kitty Darling! Darling Patrick!

Patrick I say! Good grief! What on earth do you think you're doing, Kitty? Look out—you'll have me on my back.

Kitty I've dreamed of this, Patrick. (*She rolls on top of him*)

Patrick Get off me, Kitty. You can't roll about on the carpet at seven in the evening.

Kitty Surrender.

Patrick What do you mean?

Kitty Surrender. Submit. Relax.

Patrick All right, I submit. Now let me get up.

Kitty After you've kissed me.

Patrick Now look here.

Kitty I said kiss me.

Patrick And then you'll let me get up?

Kitty If you still want to.

They kiss

Oh, Patrick.

The door opens. Hedwig enters followed by Jack in an impeccable denim suit. He is a rather intimidatingly precise and proper young man of twenty-two

Hedwig In here, Jack. We won't be disturbed. Oh, mein Gott! So sorry!

Jack Evening, Father.

Patrick and Kitty sit up on the floor

Patrick Why, Jack.

Hedwig I'm sorry, I thought you were in the garden.

Patrick No, no, we came in.

Jack Are you all right down there?

Patrick Splendid, fine, we're just gathering matches. Look, there's one of the cunning little blighters over there.

Jack I shouldn't bother about that for the moment.

Patrick What?

Jack Our guest.

Patrick What?

Jack I don't believe I've met our guest.

Patrick Oh. Oh, no. This is Kitty. Stand up, Kitty. Mrs Tansy. This is Jack, my son.

Kitty Oh, the agricultural college, yes. (*She gets up and shakes hands*)

Patrick Cirencester.

Jack How do you do, Kitty.

Kitty How do you do, Jack.

Jack I'm glad you picked such a lovely weekend.

Kitty It's one out of the bag.

Jack And how are you, Father?

Patrick Never better.

Jack Tuck your shirt in. Where's Mother?

Hedwig She's chopping herbs in the kitchen. I'll tell her you've arrived. Excuse, please. (*She goes to the door*)

Kitty And I'll run up and change my tights. I've got a ladder that goes all the way from the knee right up——

Patrick Yes, yes, see you later, Kitty.

Hedwig After you, madam.

Kitty Oh, thank you, Hedwig.

Kitty and Hedwig leave

Patrick (*going to the drinks*) Would you like a snifter?

Jack Were you assaulting that woman?

Patrick Absolutely not. I'm snow white over the whole affair. I'll have one myself if you don't mind. (*He pours a large drink*)

Jack It didn't look like a hunt for matches.

Patrick No.

Jack You were locked in each other's arms.

Patrick Yes, but I was underneath.

Jack I don't see what difference that makes.

Patrick It made a difference to me. I couldn't get out.

Jack Are you saying she forced her attentions on you?

Patrick Exactly.

Jack Do you often have that effect on women?

Patrick Not all that often. (*After a pause*) It's never happened before, to be perfectly honest. Jack, do I write a good letter?

Jack You?

Patrick Yes, do I write a good one?

Jack No.

Patrick Apparently her head's been turned by my sublime prose style.

Bethany comes in and rushes up to kiss Jack

Bethany Jack, my dear, how good to see you.

Jack Hello, Mother.

Bethany Have you met our guests?

Jack Only Kitty.

Bethany Oh, yes, I sent Ted out to cut some rosemary. Mr Bithynian.

Jack Come again?

Bethany Ted Bithynian. How did you find Kitty?

Jack Rolling on the carpet with Father.

Bethany Don't you think her hair's just like a copper beech in a September sunset? Rolling on the carpet?

Patrick She assaulted me. I'm snow white over the whole affair.

Bethany Kitty made advances?

Patrick I was on my back before I knew what had hit me.

Bethany How absolutely extraordinary.

Patrick That she should find me attractive?

Bethany Ted made overtures to me.

Patrick Well, I'm damned.

Bethany Is it so inconceivable?

Jack Would you mind explaining what's happening?

Bethany Those poor creatures.

Patrick Eh?

Bethany Simply crying out for affection. So starved of love that at the
   first sign of kindness they simply lose control. They're like kittens that
   you take in from the cold. In no time at all they're rubbing up against
   you and purring.

Patrick Kitty.

Bethany What?

Patrick Like a pussy. Kitty.

Bethany Kinder to drown unwanted pussycats at birth. That's always been
   your view, hasn't it, Jack?

Patrick I remember Sukie's last litter. You sat there with your hands
   plunged in the bucket.

Bethany Up to your elbows, Jack. Sleeves rolled up.

Jack I'd hardly leave them down.

Patrick Watching the Test Match on television.

Bethany So patient and gentle and firm. Not one splash. First one and
   then another and then another.

Patrick The fast merchants were bowling. You gave each kitten one over.
   Do you remember?

Jack Alan Knott scored ninety.

Bethany And then there was your pet duck.

Jack Davinia?

Bethany I'll always remember what you said when Davinia stopped
   laying.

Jack Neck it.

Patrick And neck it you did, Jack.

Jack You can't afford sentiment. It destroys you.

Bethany We tried to bring you up to be realistic.

Patrick Nothing soft about our Jack.

Bethany So you'd survive in the cold unemotional times we could see
   coming.

Patrick Not spoilt like our parents spoiled us.

Bethany We're still squeamish about the more, well, down-to-earth
   aspects of farming.

Patrick Mother means slaughtering. Can't even say it. Ha-ha.

Jack All this is leading somewhere. (*After a pause*) Do you want me to
   slaughter something? Is it Clarissa?

Bethany No! Jack, how could you dream of such a thing? She's still
   giving the most beautiful milk.

28

Pen-Friends

Jack Less than a gallon a day, Mother.

Bethany Never mind Clarissa. We asked you home this weekend for a purpose.

Patrick Yes, we're getting sidetracked. Can I tell you an instructive story, Jack? Is there time before dinner?

Bethany We'll have to make it, won't we?

Patrick There was once a man living in the country. A painter of landscapes. A townsman in fact, but he was seeking the time and tranquillity to create works of a higher order. Or so his country neighbours imagined.

Bethany Because in reality, Jack, he was——

Patrick Let me tell it, darling. In reality he was not a painter. Our man had been bowlerhatted by the army. There were plenty of good men on the scrapheap in those days. At all events, he ended up as a salesman selling a spiv exterior wall-coating that self-destructed to coincide with the customers' last payment. He wasn't one of your flashy door-to-door men, mind you. He sold to big corporations and town councils and a prison or two. Anybody with a large stretch of wall that needed coating.

Jack This is before he lived in the country?

Patrick Yes. One day they sent him to a cathedral to sell his dreadful wall-coating and he said to himself, "What in the name of the prophet am I doing?" He went back to the marketing manager. He said: "This is worse than dishonest, it's sacrilege." The marketing manager said, "Get it tied up fast because something red hot's just come in for you—a string of orphanages." Our man went home. He did a lot of thinking on the way home. He went home and told his wife he'd made a packet on the stock market; £90,000, they could afford to retire, they'd buy a place in the country, he'd paint, she'd birdwatch. They would rent a country cottage for a year while they looked around for a permanent place.

Jack Did he believe all this himself?

Patrick Believe it?

Jack He was having a breakdown.

Patrick No. Not at all.

Jack I got the impression he was skint.

Patrick They sold their house in the suburbs and rented a farmhouse in Anglesey. He reckoned their money would last a year. Tan-y-Bryn. What a year that was. There was snow on the mountain above the house. Snow drops. What toboggan rides. He was full of his snowscapes. She was off house hunting.

Bethany There were pine fires, estate agents' particulars, friends in from the village. At the end of the lane was the Atlantic. In June the baby played in the paddock all day dressed in nothing but daisies. Baked like a harvest loaf.

Patrick He painted the young corn, the cuckoo . . . curlew . . . lapwing.

Bethany It took one year to find the house she'd been looking for.

Patrick They threw a party on the last night. Friends from the village. Grand people. They said their goodbyes and she went on to bed ahead of him. He locked up. He drained the last bottle and put the cat out. He

went on up with his revolver. She was asleep. He placed the muzzle
against her temple. (*After a pause*) She opened her eyes.

Bethany "What are you doing?" she said.

Patrick "There is no ninety thousand. I'm a skint man," he said.

Bethany "What are you going to do?" she said.

Patrick "We've had one good year. Now we pay our shot."

Betany "What are you going to do?"

Patrick "You . . . then the baby . . . then me."

Bethany "What about the insurance?" she said.

Patrick "I don't carry any."

Bethany "You absurd blighter," she said. "I mean my policy on your
life."

Patrick She hadn't told him, Jack. Fifty thousand if he died in an accident.

Bethany Wayfarers sometimes spent the night in the hayloft.

Patrick They offered one a bed in the house. A man with no appendages.

Bethany Albert Anthony Schubert.

Patrick His charred bones passed for the husband's.

Bethany It was him or the three of them, Jack. You see that? The widow
moved to Ireland. Roscommon. In time she married a Mr Schubert.

Patrick Mr Schubert was roasted three years later at a profit of ninety-four
thousand.

Bethany The widow moved to the Ngong Hills in Kenya. A coffee planta-
tion. Near Nairobi.

Jack Yes, Mother, I know. I went to school in Nairobi.

Bethany In time there was another fire. Another widow. Another pay-out
from the insurance company.

Patrick Most of it's gone, Jack.

Bethany Despite prudent management.

Patrick It kept us comfortable for sixteen years.

Bethany But you see, Jack—are you listening?

Jack Yes, Mother.

Bethany You see, new wayfarers have to be found. New people with no
appendages.

Jack Yes, I see.

Patrick Ted and Kitty.

Bethany You see, this time the pair of us are going to be found inciner-
ated.

Patrick And you'll be the beneficiary, Jack.

Bethany Two hundred and twenty-three thousand pounds.

Patrick And you can bring it to us in South Africa, where the three of us
will live very comfortably on the income.

Jack Yes, I see. What if I say no?

Patrick You'll be a skint man.

Jack I could always go farming.

Patrick Without capital?

Jack It has been known.

Patrick Yes, if you're prepared to work for twenty pounds a week, seven
days a week, fifty-two weeks a year. Never go out, be tied to a cow's

tail, never have a holiday, and the same for your wife. Well, go to it.
Go farming. Quite a lot do, and they kill themselves.

Hedwig comes in

Hedwig Excuse me, madam. Dinner will be served in five minutes.
Bethany Thank you, Hedwig. Have you told Ted and Kitty?
Hedwig They'll be down in five minutes.
Bethany We'll be in directly.
Hedwig Thank you.

Hedwig leaves

Bethany Hedwig was right. Black does become her.
Jack And where will Hedwig be while the flames are . . . leaping and
licking?
Bethany At three in the morning? In bed, I imagine.
Jack You've insured her, too?
Bethany No. These insurance people aren't complete fools.
Jack But she'll go up in smoke just the same?
Patrick We can't have her saying there were five people in the house.
Jack Didn't Ted and Kitty come by train? They must have been seen at
the Halt.
Patrick I picked them up at Oxenholme. And I went in disguise.
Jack And when does the fire break out?
Patrick Tonight.
Bethany Three o'clock in the morning. Are you with us, Jack?

Jack takes a slow turn up and down the room

Jack (*finally facing them*) Do you honestly expect me to go along with
this? Without thinking it over?
Bethany How long do you need?
Jack Three lives are at stake, that's all. I mean, that's all, Mother.
Bethany Yes, I see that. Well, how long would you like?
Jack Two hours.
Patrick That's fair enough.
Bethany Don't rush into a decision you'd regret. And now we must go
into dinner. I wouldn't like anything to get burnt.

They go out as—

the CURTAIN *slowly falls*

ACT II

The same. 10 p.m. that night

As the CURTAIN *rises Hedwig is taking coffee cups etc. from a tray and putting them on the two small tables by the armchairs. She plumps the cushions etc.*

Jack comes in, walks up behind her and puts his arms round her waist. She is obviously used to it and makes no objection

Jack Hello, my delicious Rhinemaiden.

Hedwig Ja, hello my handsome young Englander.

Jack Dinner's over.

Hedwig Good. I've just made the coffee. Could you ask them to come through?

Jack Too late will be the cry. They've already gone.

Hedwig They've gone? Where?

Jack To walk off their dinner.

Hedwig At ten o'clock?

Jack It's bright moonlight. Soft summer night. Emboldened by good wine.

Hedwig Where are they going?

Jack Oh, they'll follow the sheeptrail to the top of Bonfire Hill . . . (*He breaks off thoughtfully*)

Hedwig Yes? Something the matter?

Jack (*thoughtfully*) Bonfire Hill—always wondered where that got it's name . . . Anyway, they'll follow the sheeptrail to the top of Bonfire Hill and they'll look down on the tarn glittering in the moonlight and when they feel chilly they'll sober up and turn back. Do you mind if I kiss you?

Hedwig Not at the moment, please, darling.

Jack Home five hours and no kiss?

Hedwig There's been too much kissing in this room for one day.

Jack Ah, there can never be too much kissing.

Hedwig Ted kissing Kitty, then Ted kissing Bethany, and then Kitty kissing Patrick.

Jack Really going at it, were they? Firing on all cylinders?

Hedwig I didn't see their cylinders, but yes, I should say they were firing strongly.

Jack Wait a bit. You say Ted was kissing Kitty?

Hedwig Ja.

Jack When was this?

Hedwig About ten minutes after they arrived.

Jack But they'd never set eyes on each other before.

Hedwig I know. Short acquaintance seems to be a condition of this kissing outbreak. I daren't think what they're doing on Bonfire Hill at this moment.

Jack Hedwig, curb that Wagnerian imagination.

Hedwig In all that bracken.

Jack Don't leap to sensational conclusions.

Hedwig In the moonlight.

Jack (*amused*) For pity's sake, Hedwig. In der bracken! In der moonlight!

Hedwig Jack, I don't like being laughed at.

Jack I can't help it. When you assume that puritanical tone like some outraged female Martin Luther I just find it pricelessly funny.

Hedwig Jack!

Jack In der bracken! In der moonlight!

Hedwig What precisely do you find so amusing?

Jack I'm just reminded of the way the pair of us slip out of the house on every fine night I happen to be home.

Hedwig That is not the same.

Jack Scattering our clothes on the lower slopes.

Hedwig Jack!

Jack Firing on all cylinders.

Hedwig Enough! Silence! Mein Gott!

Jack In der bracken! In der moonlight!

Hedwig Yes, but we're young. It's taken for granted *we'll* be immoral and irresponsible and promiscuous.

Jack Don't talk wet.

Hedwig I've always regarded Bethany and Patrick as a kind of mother and father. I expect them to set a moral example.

Jack Don't talk wet. Since when have morals mattered to us?

Hedwig Exactly. Shut up and listen. We have no morals and that's splendid and fine and liberating and life-entrancing. We can do exactly as we please without being burdened with the slightest feeling of guilt.

Jack But?

Hedwig An absence of morals is no good if it exists in a vacuum. We need good people around us to bounce our immorality off. And now I find that Bethany and Patrick are just as immoral as we are.

Jack Oh, every bit, but not in the way you mean.

Hedwig No?

Jack You'd be surprised. Do you know where Father's binoculars are?

Hedwig The desk, lower right-hand drawer. Why do you want binoculars?

Jack Just want to cast an eye over Bonfire Hill. (*He finds the binoculars and stands in the window looking out*)

Hedwig Spy? You want to spy on your parents', er, honky-tonky?

Jack Hanky-panky, darling.

Hedwig You're nothing but a nasty sneaking Peeping Tim.

Jack Ah, come out here, Hedwig. Balmy, velvety, delicious. I never saw the sky so thickly crusted with stars.

Hedwig Jack, put those binoculars down.

Jack Sublime. You can see every bracken frond and every ball of sheep-dung. You can practically see a fly crawling up the Langdale Pikes.

Hedwig Come inside and drink your coffee.

Jack Wait. I've zoomed in on the most beautiful lady sheep. Moonlight becomes ewe. Hello? There goes a big buck hare hopping down the sheeptrail. Moonlight becomes ewe, it goes with your hare. I'll have to send that one to the *Beano*.

Hedwig Isn't that where it came from? Now put those binoculars down before you see something that could mutilate you.

Jack Ah, there they are! Exactly as I thought.

Hedwig What? You mean . . .?

Jack Yes, the four of them.

Hedwig Are they—are they . . .?

Jack Oh, very close together, yes. A very intimate group. Oh, dear. Here. Have a look.

Hedwig No, Jack. Keep those filthy glasses to yourself.

Jack My word, yes, they're on top of one another, in a manner of speaking. But then it's a very small bench.

Hedwig Bench?

Jack Yes, that bench on top of the hill.

Hedwig What are they doing . . . on a bench?

Jack Sitting side by side. What else?

Hedwig What else?

Jack Yes, why, you didn't think they'd be—good heavens, Hedwig, you didn't imagine——

Hedwig Don't try to be funny. Give me those glasses.

Jack Careful. Don't snatch.

Hedwig I can't see anything. They don't fit my eyes.

Jack Bend them together.

Hedwig Ah, that's better.

Jack I can see them with the naked eye now, if you'll pardon the phrase. Silhouetted. Right on top. Have you got them?

Hedwig Ah!

Jack What are they doing now?

Hedwig (*disappointed*) As you say, side by side, admiring the tarn. Quite close but quite innocent. Ah!

Jack Yes?

Hedwig Patrick is reddening his pipe. Ah, puff puff. Now he stands. They all stand. They're coming down. They feel the chill.

Jack And so do I. (*He moves back into the room*)

Hedwig I'll make some fresh coffee.

Jack Just a minute, Hedwig. Before they get here.

Hedwig Yes?

Jack Are you serious about me?

Hedwig Serious?

Jack Love—passion—total commitment. Are you serious?

Hedwig Oh, that.

Jack Yes.

Hedwig Well . . . what a curious time to ask.

Jack Are you?

Hedwig I want to sleep with you and have your children and bake your bread, yes. (*After a pause*) I think you should kiss me now.

He gives her a quick pecking kiss

Jack I'm sorry, there's no time to give you a proper one at the moment. Listen, this has got to be quick.

Hedwig I do love you, Jack.

Jack Bugger it, woman, shut up and listen. Mother and Father are proposing to burn the house down and kill Ted and Kitty, have you got that?

Hedwig Why?

Jack So their insurance company will think the charred bodies are those of Mother and Father and hand me two hundred and twenty-three thousand pounds, which I will later split with them in South Africa. Got it?

Hedwig Yes.

Jack What do you think of it?

Hedwig Very good.

Jack You approve?

Hedwig If it makes you rich.

Jack You've got no weak-minded scruples about that sort of thing?

Hedwig My mind is strong.

Jack Yet you still have these strange sexual taboos.

Hedwig My mind is strong.

Jack You haven't let me go all the way with you.

Hedwig As I say, my mind is strong.

Jack But you approve of Father and Mother's plan?

Hedwig Provided all the tracks are covered.

Jack There's just one drawback as far as you're concerned.

Hedwig Oh?

Jack They want to burn you to ashes as well.

Hedwig (*after a long open-mouthed pause*) I'll go and make some more coffee.

Jack You're offended, aren't you?

Hedwig No, no.

Jack You mustn't take it personally.

Hedwig No? I'm just to be barbecued in my bed?

Jack There's no need to get shirty.

Hedwig But I thought Bethany and Patrick were fond of me.

Jack They are fond of you. They regard you almost like a daughter. Almost.

Hedwig Then why?

Jack It will look more convincing if one of the bodies isn't insured.

Hedwig They haven't insured me?

Jack They won't make a penny out of your death.

Hedwig Well, that's almost altruistic.

Jack Don't let it embitter your feelings for them.

Hedwig I'll try not to.

Jack Remember all the happy times you've had together. Don't let resentment spoil these last few hours.

Hedwig These last few hours?

Jack Yes. Mother and Father will be dead by morning.

Hedwig Bethany and Patrick will be dead?

Jack Peace be to their ashes.

Hedwig Their ashes?

Jack For pity's sake, Hedwig, sometimes I have a tiny feeling that your obtuseness is just a masquerade. Must I spell out every syllable.

Hedwig Yes please.

Jack Mother and Father will be roasted in their four-poster. The money will be all mine. Every penny.

Hedwig Isn't that rather selfish?

Jack Oh, I'll share it with you.

Hedwig Aren't you fond of your mother and father?

Jack Fond? Mother and Father make me furious. They're the most superfluous couple I've ever encountered. They exist purely to feed their banal appetites. When I come back to this place and see the bracken smothering good grazing land, when I see the water courses choked with the roots of old trees, I literally froth at the mouth. I could squash them like slugs. Tweed-suited slugs. Purposeless parasites, that's what they are. A gentleman farmer, he has the nerve to call himself. Do you know what a gentleman farmer is? A gentleman farmer is somebody who shows his animals to his friends and his friends to his animals once a week and never dirties his hands. And their squalid pursuit of more money! Do you know, I sometimes suspect they'd go to any lengths to get it. More money to do what? To squander on dahlias and azalias and line their sleek paunches. Not to keep the land in good heart. They could have made a go of this place with all the thousands they've netted but they're bone idle. If only they'd bred a pedigree herd, if they'd mended their fences, if they'd trimmed and laid their hedges, if they'd cleared their copses and grown some decent timber—oh, if Father had even learned to turn out a decent picture, the poor man's still painting by numbers. The entirely spurious Silverlocks. They resort to murder like a P. G. Wodehouse drone who taps a nutty uncle and blows all the proceeds on gin fizzes and silk pyjamas. I don't know, perhaps I'm old-fashioned, but to me murder for profit is only legitimate as long as one puts the profit to good account.

Hedwig Jack, I do believe you're an actual puritan at heart. What will *you* do with the money?

Jack I'll rebuild the house. Grapple with the land. I'll manure it liberally, oh, I'll manure it liberally and make it sweet and fertile. Raise good hardy stock. But not a gentleman farmer. Never that. No. A farming gentleman. And given a reasonable climate and a decent Government subsidy, a good price for wool, I don't see why we shouldn't be able to survive without murder for years and years.

Hedwig takes a slow turn up and down, then puts a question

Hedwig What will you do about Ted and Kitty?
Jack There's a swamp in the bottom meadow. You know it? Covered in slime—Jinny Greenteeth. We lost a cow in it once. They won't be found.

Hedwig goes up to him and loops her arms about his neck

Hedwig Oh, Jack, I do love you.
Jack You'd better.
Hedwig May I have that proper kiss now?

They kiss

    Bethany comes in through the french windows followed by Patrick, Kitty and Ted

Bethany (*as she enters*) The fragrance of the azaleas is overpowering, isn't it, Patrick? Oh! Hello, dear.
Jack (*startled*) Oh, hello, Mother.
Hedwig (*startled*) Good evening, madam.
Ted (*slightly tipsy*) Hello! So this is why Master Jack missed out on the walkie-walkies.
Kitty Ted, don't be . . . indelicate.
Ted Sorry, sorry, sorry. My feeble attempt at fun, Kitty.
Kitty Very.
Patrick Ah, coffee. Do I spy coffee?
Hedwig I was about to make some more, sir. I'm afraid that will be cold. (*She picks up the tray with the coffee pot*)
Patrick Ah, yes, good idea.
Hedwig If you'll excuse me.

Hedwig goes to the door and Jack follows

Jack I'll come with you. Excuse me.

    Hedwig and Jack leave

Ted Shall I tell you something? She didn't keep the coffee hot but she certainly had your lad on the boil.
Kitty Ted, didn't that walk sober you up? I don't know, he's always the same after . . . (*She stops dead*)
Bethany Yes, Kitty?
Kitty Well, he just strikes me as the type of man who runs to vulgarity when he's taken a drop too much.
Patrick (*amused*) Good heavens, no falling out, you two. You sound just like an old married couple.

Ted and Kitty roar with laughter

    What? I say, did I make a good joke?
Kitty (*laughing*) Old married couple!
Ted Fantastic!

Patrick You see, Bethany? Bethany always says my jokes are hopeless. Says they're not fit to print in the *Beano*. Tell you a secret? I wasn't even trying that time.

Kitty I hope I'm there when you are.

Ted We'll collapse all over the place.

Kitty But seriously, Bethany, aren't you a tiny bit worried . . . about that developing? Your Jack and that girl?

Bethany Oh, no, I can't see it lasting, somehow. Can you, Patrick?

Patrick Not for long.

Kitty I mean, she is a domestic after all and you know what they say about gold-digging au pairs. You can't be too careful these days.

Ted You never know who's trying to diddle you.

Bethany Oh, that's so cynical. Actually I think it's quite lovely. Two young people meet, thrown together by chance, and that's a miracle in itself. And then all the forces of circumstance are united against them usually and if they somehow overcome them that's another miracle. Who are we to stand against Jack and Hedwig if it's so ordained in Heaven? I know Patrick agrees with me.

Patrick Absolutely. It's all in God's hands. Where did I put those matches? Ah, in my pocket all the time.

Ted Bethany, you're such a good and trusting soul, it would almost be a crime to open your eyes to all the wickedness floating about.

Bethany It's just that these young people have all their lives before them and we've had our innings. If we were to die in our beds tonight we couldn't have any complaints.

Ted What? Throw in the towel? Give up the ghost? A beautiful and sensitive young woman like you? Listen, you could still bring somebody enormous happiness, you know.

Kitty No, I know just how she feels. On a night like this you get . . . a sense of completion. Peace. Harmony with nature. The stars close enough to touch. I could almost die happily in this place and become one with the landscape. I could rest happily buried among all this peace and beauty.

Patrick Wouldn't you rather be cremated?

Jack comes in, followed by Hedwig with the coffee

Jack Coffee is served. In you go, Hedwig.

Hedwig Thank you, sir.

The others react with: "That smells good", "Piping hot", "Fantastic!", "Just the ticket" etc. as Hedwig pours the coffee

Jack Shall I hand them round? (*Offering Kitty a cup*) There you are, Kitty.

Kitty Thank you, Jack.

Jack Cream? Sugar?

Ted She's slimming.

Jack Oh? Mother?

Bethany Thank you, darling.

Jack And what have you been talking about?
Patrick Cremation.

Hedwig bangs down the coffee pot violently

Hedwig Mein Gott!
Jack Hedwig, are you OK?
Hedwig Just the lid slipped, that's all, no damage.

Jack gives her a look, then resumes his task

Jack Here you are, Father.
Patrick Thank you, my boy. (*He drinks*) Yes, Kitty was saying she fancied being buried in one of our fields.

Hedwig knocks over a cup

Jack (*laughing with an edge*) Hedwig! Butterfingers.
Hedwig So clumsy. Mein Gott.
Patrick Yes, I've always favoured cremation, personally.
Jack That's looking a long time ahead, Father, one hopes.
Bethany Well, I'm like Kitty. When my time comes I want to be buried.
Jack That's going to be awkward.
Bethany Oh yes, I see what you mean. With Father being cremated. Yes, I suppose you'd better commit us both to the flames, darling.
Hedwig Will you excuse me, please, madam?
Bethany Is anything wrong, Hedwig?
Hedwig I'm sorry, but I find this conversation a little distasteful.
Ted Oh, come on, girl, these matters have to be ventilated.
Hedwig I don't honestly see why.
Kitty It's always a wise precaution, dear—to let somebody know your preference before it's too late.
Patrick (*anxious and solicitous*) You don't object to cremation *per se*, do you, little Hedwig?
Hedwig Yes.
Bethany Oh, dear.
Hedwig (*with an edge of hysteria*) I belong to a small but strict Bavarian Baptist sect which considers cremation, er, fatal—fatal to the survival of the soul.
Patrick Is there no dispensation if you die abroad?
Hedwig None.
Bethany (*looking at Patrick*) Oh, dear, that is a nuisance.
Kitty Goodness, it is getting cold. I should have worn a cardigan over this sleeveless dress. Patrick, just feel the goose pimples at the top of my arm.
Patrick (*escaping*) Er, I'll switch the heating on, shall I? It's a topcoat colder up here. (*He goes to the radiator switch*)
Bethany Yes, do, Patrick. One thing I can promise Kitty, you won't be cold in bed.
Kitty I'm sure I won't. What a snug little bedroom.
Bethany I hope the bars at the window don't spoil the view. It used to be Jack's room when he was little.

Kitty Nursery bars? Why are they made of steel?
Jack I was a very strong little boy.
Ted I've got bars at my windows, as well.
Jack I used to walk in my sleep.
Patrick There. The heating's coming on. Can you feel it?
Kitty That's gorgeous.
Ted What have you got? Solid fuel?
Patrick Oil, actually.
Ted I didn't spot the tank.
Patrick No, you wouldn't.
Bethany An oil tank's such an appalling eyesore, especially in the country, don't you think?
Jack Especially one that holds two thousand gallons.
Bethany Patrick very cleverly tucked it out of sight.
Ted Oh, where?
Patrick Inside the house, actually.
Ted Inside the house? Whereabouts?
Bethany An old store-room we never use.
Ted (*laughing*) As long as it isn't next to our bedrooms!
Patrick It's underneath them, actually.

Ted and Kitty roar with laughter

Ted Underneath them! What a sense of humour!
Patrick I say, did I make another good joke?
Kitty (*laughing*) It's just the po-faced way they pop out.
Ted (*laughing*) Underneath the bedrooms! What will he come up with next?
Patrick Well what would you say to a brandy?
Ted Fantastic!
Kitty Only I warn you, I'll sleep the sleep of the dead.
Hedwig Shall I make them, sir?
Patrick No, no, sit down, one of the family.

Everyone settles down comfortably as Patrick deals with the drinks

Kitty You know, that's what I love about this place. One of the family. Even a little waif like me.
Ted Fantastic.
Kitty This feeling of total acceptance. You don't find it these days.
Patrick (*offering Kitty a drink*) There you are, my dear.
Kitty Oh, what an enormous drink! Are you trying to knock me out?
Ted I'll tell you what. I'll tell you what. If only the whole world——
Patrick (*offering a drink*) Ted?
Ted Oh, cheers, Patrick. (*He drinks and gasps*) Hell's teeth! You'll have me blistered! No, if all the people in the world could all sit down like this and bury their hatchets, with no aggro and no ulterior motives— you know?
Patrick A drink for you, Bethany?
Bethany Not for me, dear.

Ted All sitting down in harmony like we are now——
Patrick Hedwig? Will you join us?
Hedwig Thank you.
Ted Because what's been lost in this sort of headlong race to get your paws on more than the next man——
Patrick Jack?
Jack Thanks.
Ted What's been lost is simple trust and old-fashioned British decency.
Patrick Hear-hear.
Ted Because I'll tell you what. (*He drinks*) It's nice to be nice, isn't it?
Patrick Let me top you up, Ted. (*He splashes more into Ted's glass*)
Ted Know what I mean? It's nice to be nice. Cheers! (*He drinks*)

The others ad lib: "Cheers!"

Patrick Well, that calls for another drink.

Patrick starts topping the others up. All of them make laughing protests

Ted A toast! A toast to our hospit—our hospit——
Patrick No, no, no, we'll toast you. Here, Bethany, just take this little drink.
Bethany No, really, Patrick.
Patrick Bethany, we're going to *toast* Ted and Kitty.
Bethany Oh yes, all right, dear.
Patrick Ted and Kitty!

Both raise their glasses

Bethany Ted and Kitty!
Jack And now it's our turn. Hedwig?
Hedwig Yes, Jack?
Jack We're going to toast Father and Mother, aren't we?
Hedwig Oh—oh, yes.
Jack Father and Mother!

Jack raises his glass and Hedwig follows

Hedwig Bethany and Patrick!
Bethany Oh, the darlings.

The doorbell rings

   (*Tensely*) Patrick, did I hear . . .?
Patrick (*tensely*) The doorbell.

The doorbell rings again

   Hedwig?
Hedwig Yes. Yes, at once.

   Hedwig goes out

Ted Doorbell? 'Leven at night? Up here?
Patrick Please be quiet, Ted.

Hedwig's and Bill's voices are heard indistinctly outside. The conversation lasts a full twenty seconds and the others stare at the door

   Hedwig returns at last

   Well?

Hedwig Patrick, I think you'd better come and deal with this.
Patrick Who is it?
Hedwig It's a man with a bicycle.
Patrick (*after a pause*) Well—give him a glass of water and get rid of him.
Hedwig He says his name is Bill.
Patrick Bill?

   Bill enters with a rucksack on his back and a bunch of flowers in his hand. He is a Cockney aged sixty

Bill (*as he enters; cheerfully*) Ah-ah. Sorry to barge in at this late hour. Evening, all. I hope you'll excuse my bare knees.
Patrick (*bemused*) Bill?
Bill Damn fine splendid! You remember me!
Patrick Bill who?
Bill Don't tell me you've forgotten old Bill.
Patrick I've never set eyes on you. I think you've got a hell of a nerve.
Bill Well, strike a light, if you'll pardon the expression.
Patrick We're waiting for you to go. Get out. What was that you said?
Bill Said? when?
Patrick Just now. This minute.
Bill I don't get you.
Patrick Would you mind repeating what you just said?
Bill Repeating? Er, well . . . oh, yes. Nothing very memorable. I said, "Ah-ah, sorry to barge in at this disgraceful time of night." That what you mean?
Patrick No—no. After.
Bill Oh, wait, yes. I apologized for the bare knees. I'm on a cycling holiday. CTC badge, see? Youth Hostels Association? Can't remember how I put it exactly. Look, is this crucial?
Bethany (*dangerously calm*) He said, "Well, strike a light, if you'll forgive the expression."
Bill (*recognizing her*) Bethany! Popsicle! Don't tell me *you've* forgotten old Bill. Look. I picked you a posy.
Bethany Bill who?
Bill Bill Kemp. Bill Kemp! Oh, your memory's bad but your beauty's unfading, Bethany.
Patrick We're waiting for you to leave.
Bill Is he kidding?
Patrick Get out of my house! Leave! Scram! Go!

Pause. Then Kitty utters a drunken giggle

Bill (*pathetically*) OK . . . OK . . . sorry . . . I've made an error, haven't I? Suppose I must look ridiculous. I'm sixty, you know. Covered in dust. Legs too *white* for khaki cycling shorts, aren't they? Always did lack three or four of the social graces. Pot belly. Silly of me to expect a warm welcome. We kid ourselves we've got real friends, don't we, and we mean no more to them than that. (*He snaps his fingers*)

Patrick Good-night!

Bill Well, you'll take this off my hands, Bethany? Little posy I picked by moonlight. Plundered the hedge coming up the hill, beg its pardon.

Bethany No, please, just go.

Bill You can at least give *these* a drink.

Bethany Very well. (*She accepts the bouquet*)

Bill See? Mountain geranium, bird cherry, forget-me-nots, buttercups, lilac, bluebells, yellow poppy, kingcups, speedwell . . .

Bethany Yes, Mr Kemp.

Bill Mind you, nothing like the flowers that grew in the Ngong hills. Those massive giant lillies.

Patrick Ngong Hills?

Bill But I can see I've outstayed my welcome. I'll say goodnight. (*He turns to go*)

Patrick No, just one moment, Mr—ah—Bill.

Bill Yes?

Bethany The Ngong Hills? (*She gives a small laugh*)

Bill I say something funny?

Patrick No, it's just that—ha-ha—it's so remiss of us to fail to recognize such a . . .

Bill Get off! You've twigged me?

Patrick The dear old Ngong Hills upon my word.

Bethany Close the door, Bill. Come and sit down.

Jack Let me relieve you of your rucksack, Mr Kemp.

Bill Oh, very good of you. Weight off my shoulders.

Jack (*taking the rucksack*) Yes. I say, this is heavy. I'm Jack.

Bill Very pleased.

Jack (*introducing*) Kitty Tansy—Ted Bithynian.

Bill Evening all. (*After a pause*) Bithynian . . . Bithynian . . . Haven't we met before?

Ted Not as far as I know.

Jack And Hedwig of course you've met.

Bill Exactly.

Jack Sit down, Mr Kemp.

Bill Thanks.

Jack Yes, it's not many people who remember Mother and Father from their days in the Ngong Hills.

Bill You know, I shouldn't be surprised if I'm the last. They kept themselves very much to themselves.

Jack Father, you know what I think?

Patrick What's that, Jack?

Jack I think we should toast Mr Kemp.

Patrick That's exactly what I was thinking. (*He gives a short laugh*) Where's the bottle? (*He picks up one but finds it empty*) Hello? This is a dead man. Have to open another, but never fear, never fear, everything must go. (*He gets a fresh bottle from the sideboard*)

Bethany To be honest, Bill, I must confess I still can't quite . . .

Bill No, I never make a lasting impression.

Bethany What exactly were you doing in Africa?

Bill Oh, just prospecting.

Bethany Diamonds?

Bill Digging for this and that.

Bethany With any success?

Bill I never did turn up exactly what I was after. Trail went cold. The boys in Nairobi are still looking. Hello, there's a match on the carpet. Near your chair, Mr Bithynian.

Ted All right, I've got it. Been turning up all over the room.

Patrick Kitty, let me fill you up.

Kitty (*with drunken elaboration*) Thank you, Patrick.

Patrick Bethany?

Bethany Just a tiny one. (*To Bill*) Did you spend a long time in the Ngong Hills?

Bill Only a few weeks. I couldn't stand the heat.

Patrick Ted? Top you up?

Bill Didn't it get too hot for you in the end?

Patrick is startled and pours drink on Ted's trousers

Ted Hell's teeth, Patrick!

Patrick I'm sorry, Ted.

Ted All over my slacks.

Patrick You won't be needing them tomorrow.

Ted Won't be needing . . . (*Laughing*) Won't be needing my slacks! Did you hear that one, Kitty?

Kitty (*laughing*) I don't know where he gets it from. Don't you find him a scream, Bill?

Bill I've often speculated on what makes people laugh.

Kitty (*very drunkenly serious*) Oh? Speculated?

Bill Yes and I've got this theory.

Kitty Oh? Theory make us laugh?

Bill That's right.

Kitty Oh? Listen to this, Ted. Theory make us laugh.

Bill Why do we laugh?

Kitty (*respectfully*) Go on then. We're listening.

Bill People say something unexpected and it makes you cold inside, so you cough.

Kitty Cough? (*After a pause*) Cough! I get it!

Ted Oh, my godfathers!

Ted and Kitty roar with laughter

Patrick On that happy note, on that happy note, a toast to Bill.

All, except Bill, raise their glasses, ad lib: *"To Bill" and then drink*

I say, Bill, I never gave you a drink.

Bill That's OK, I never drink on holiday.

Kitty giggles

What I mean—you don't need it up here. I don't want my senses dulled up here. I can drink life neat up here. Wonderful! Even the silage up here—have you noticed? I love the smell of silage. Good silage. Some smells like opening a tobacco pouch. Some smells like dead rats. Some smells as sour as pig muck. Not up here. Everything you see up here makes for greatness and freedom. You can stand and watch the strange terrible heart of things visibly beating, as the poet says. You know what I feel when I come up here? Here I am, where I ought to be. Now the city, that's another story, London is, that madly-rattling Smartie tube.

Bethany You work in London, do you?

Bill All foulness congregates in the capital. Well, most of it, eh, Patrick?

Patrick It's certainly a healthy life.

Bill Just you and the sheep? Ready for fleecing, I see.

Patrick Any time now.

Bill And lambs for the slaughter?

Patrick Some of them.

Bill But that's nature. Mostly. Now I'm a town boy myself. Born in Stepney, nightschool in Willesden. I used to think flowers was a brew of beer. I used to think birds were for chatting up. I used to think the green belt was a high rank in judo, but we're all just one or two grandads from the land. Yes, this place feels like home. This house. Look at that. (*He knocks on the wood panelling*) Solid polished oak-panelling. I should judge that's been here since about sixteen sixty-six, year of the great fire of London. But this'll last for ever. (*He knocks on the wood*) Solid. Mind you, once it did catch light it'd go up like mad. Tarred beams, see? I've cased a few country-houses in my time.

Ted You've done what?

Bill I've inspected quite a few happy rural seats. But it's not every day you meet panelling like that. (*He knocks on the wood*) Hello? Did you hear that? (*He knocks on the wood*) Hollow. This section's hollow. Listen. (*He knocks on the wood*) Now I expected that. D'you know what's behind here? Ever had a peep behind this panelling?

Bethany We wouldn't dream of tampering with the fabric.

Patrick This house is a sacred trust.

Bill No harm in taking a little panel out for a peep behind. Would you just pass my rucksack, Jack?

Jack Right. Here you are.

Bill Behind this piece I think you'll find—(*taking the rucksack*) oh, thanks, Jack. (*He takes a crowbar and hammer from the rucksack*) Here we are.

Jack What's that? A crowbar?

Bill That's right.

Jack Do you always take a crowbar on your cycling holidays?

Bill That's right. (*He starts tearing out a panel with the crowbar*)

Patrick I say, what are you doing?

Bill (*taking out a panel*) Now behind this piece of panel ...

Bethany Patrick, are you going to simply watch him tear the house to pieces?

Patrick I say, Bill, that's a priceless antique you're mucking about with.

Kitty (*laughing*) I hope it's insured.

Bill (*straining*) One more good heave. There! Got it!

A big section of panelling comes down and dust fills the air. There is an assortment of coughing, shouting and laughter from everybody

Well, bless my heart and soul! There she is. Come and have a look.

Kitty What is it? A skeleton?

Bill It's an inglenook, my girl.

Patrick Well, if you're expecting us to say thank you——

Bill A beautiful inglenook! Damn fine splendid! Hedwig. Come here, Hedwig. Behold this treasure.

Hedwig Ingle *nook*?

Bill This used to be the focus of the domestic activities of the household. The symbol of the family, bearing all the traditions of the hearth. Here I am, where I ought to be! I'd have all the panelling out on this wall. There! (*He pulls more panels down*) See? You can push 'em over with your bare hand once you've got rid of one.

Bethany (*angrily*) But what if we don't want an inglenook?

Kitty laughs hysterically

Bill You know, that's thirsty work, plaster gets in the throat. I think I'll break my rule and have that drink.

Patrick I'm going to kick this nincompoop out.

Jack Don't be too hasty, Father. Remember, things will look different in the morning.

Patrick Yes, there is that.

Jack Sit down, everybody. Relax, unwind.

Bill (*sitting*) Ah, that's comfy. This is what you call a Chesterfield isn't it? It's out of place in a room like this, if you don't mind a personal observation, but I think I might keep it.

Bethany How very tolerant of you.

Patrick Here, let me fill you up. Kitty?

Kitty Thank you.

Patrick dispenses drinks

Patrick Bethany?

Bethany Oh, very well.

Patrick Hedwig?

Hedwig Danka schoen.

Patrick Ted?

Ted Fantastic.

Patrick Jack?

Jack Thank you, Father.

Patrick (*grudgingly*) And a glass for you, Bill.

Bill Happy days! Yes, I'd keep the Chesterfield. Hello, there's another match on the floor.

Ted Just a minute, Bill. Something I meant to ask you.

Bill Yes, Ted?

Ted That inglenook. I mean, you didn't just stumble across it by accident, did you?

Bill No, Ted, I had inside information. I'd keep the Chesterfield but all that china would have to go. Spode's the wrong period.

Ted Inside information?

Bill To tell you the truth, my wife Nellie and me, we've been collecting the kind of article this place needs. Old iron firedogs . . . spears, guns and pistols for the walls . . . lanterns, rushlight holders, pewter plates . . .

Ted Do you realize? This bloke carries a crowbar.

Bill A pair of lovely old armchairs—oak-ornamented with armorial quarterings.

Ted Inside information and a crowbar. Casing country-houses. Now hold on.

Bill Now what are you insinuating, Ted?

Ted Only this; that you entered this house under false colours with intent to pilfer, burgle or loot.

Bethany Is this true?

Ted He digs up some sketchy scrap of information about your past life in the Goolagong Hills and comes here trading on your good nature and gullibility and masquerading as a long lost chum. Well, just ask him what else he knows about you and see *his* memory suddenly go blank.

Patrick All right, Bill?

Bill (*after a pause*) Right. Tan-y-bryn, Anglesey, nineteen sixty, Albert Anthony Schubert. Roscommon, Eire, nineteen sixty-three, Michael Finglass Burns. Ngong Hills, Kenya, nineteen sixty-six, Sidney Van Estoop.

Pause

Ted (*laughing*) Patrick! Bethany! There's no need to sit there with your eyes popping. It still doesn't prove he knows you. Any con man can lay his hands on that kind of information about anybody. He could do the same thing with me.

Bill And Kitty.

Ted Yes, and Kitty.

Bill I've got a few notes on Kitty.

Kitty A few notes on me?

Bill (*getting out a pocket diary*) If you don't mind me referring to my Cyclists' Touring Club diary. Here we are. Colonel Podge Bentley, Clapham, Yorkshire, one thousand five hundred pounds. Mr John Tarleton, Hindhead, Surrey, three thousand pounds—still paying. Alfred John Chumcliffe, Congleton, Cheshire, racehorse breeder, two thousand guineas. Vernon Xavier O'Dowda——

Kitty moans and faints back in her chair

I'm sorry, Ted, your wife seems to have passed out.

Ted My what? My wife?

Bill The one who's just slumped sideways. You'll find a bottle of smelling salts in the outer pocket of my rucksack. Wave them gently under her nose, and meanwhile we'll pass on to you.

Patrick One moment. You say this man is that woman's husband?

Bill That's right. Normally, of course, they operate independently.

Patrick Doing what?

Bill Compromising a member of the opposite sex—always a married one, mind—and then levying blackmail, on pain of informing the third party. This time they were working in tandem, but they've gone right over the handlebars.

Kitty (*tearfully*) Patrick, don't look at me like that. There was no personal animosity intended. People have to do these things to survive.

Patrick What I find so nauseating is your cynical abuse of our hospitality.

Bill Which was to have included burning you and Ted alive, Kitty.

Kitty Burning us?

Bill The old insurance dodge.

Ted Bethany!

Bethany People have to do these things to survive, Ted. If we didn't survive we couldn't protect our children.

Bill Children in this case meaning Jack. And Jack intended doublecrossing Mum and Dad and burning them alive.

Bethany Is this true, Jack?

Patrick (*after a pause*) Don't be embarrassed, my boy. I'd have done the same myself at your age.

Jack You don't mind?

Bethany It shows you've learned to stand on your own feet.

Patrick Of course, we couldn't permit it now that we know.

Ted Patrick, if I may offer a suggestion?

Patrick Yes, Ted?

Ted We could still press ahead with your insurance scheme.

Patrick *We* could?

Ted Partners.

Patrick I'm listening.

Ted As I understand it, all we need is two bodies.

Patrick Yes.

Ted Male and female.

Patrick Yes.

Ted Bill?

Patrick Yes.

Ted (*slyly*) And one other.

Patrick Great heavens! You mean Kitty?

Ted No, no, no. What do you take me for? I don't know how to express this in the presence of the young lady herself, but it all hinges on the agreement of your boy Jack.

Kitty The au pair girl! (*She laughs*) Fantastic!

Hedwig Me? But Jack loves me, don't you, Jack? Jack?

Ted Come on, Jack, show us what you're made of.

Patrick It's up to you, my boy.

Jack Well . . .

Kitty There are plenty more where she came from. *The Daily Telegraph*'s full of them every Friday.

Jack It's not so simple . . .

Bethany Jack, dear, don't disappoint us.

Ted Come on, Jack.

Jack Well . . .

Patrick It's up to you, my boy.

Kitty Come on, be a sport.

Jack Well . . .

Patrick Yes?

Jack (*after a pause*) Well . . . All right! I'll do it!

There are various shouts of congratulations from Patrick, Bethany, Ted and Kitty

Bill Well, Bethany, I hope you're happy. You've finally brought about the total brutalization of your boy.

Bethany No, Mr Kemp, we've finally placed him beyond all harm. And now I think it's long past your bedtime, Bill. And yours, Hedwig.

Bill Is that the time already? I'll never be up in the morning.

Kitty giggles

Thank you, Kitty. Always good for a cheap laugh. Oh, before we go, I will just say that dossiers on all you ladies and gentlemen are deposited in sealed A four manilla envelopes with my old chief at Scotland Yard.

Patrick Scotland Yard?

Bill The Fraud Squad. He's going to open them if I'm not in touch tomorrow—the usual arrangement.

Bethany The Fraud Squad? You're a member of the Fraud Squad?

Bill Retired last week. Looking for a little place in the country, if you hear of anything. Something like this. Now if somebody left a deed of sale—a deed of gift—on the table of a place like this, leaving it to me and my wife Nellie, I wouldn't care what they'd done or what they did. They could go off scot free and I'd turn a blind eye. They could tootle off to that railway station and catch the first train to London after breakfast tomorrow. The ten-ten.

Patrick It's always crowded at this time of year, the ten-ten.

Bill I just happen to have five reservations in my rucksack.

Patrick Damnation, Kemp. I suppose you know that what you're suggesting—you, a police officer—is contrary to the entire spirit of the law of England?

Bill I know it, sir, and I bow my head. What I'll just say in mitigation is there's a moral four-minute mile and we're all clipping seconds off it every day, even the best of us. *My* head was turned by a corrupt young recruit to the Squad—though I blush to say it. One with a pretty face and shapely ankles and firm young ideas about the niggardly rewards a man like me can expect after a lifetime spent upholding the law. I refer to my wife Nellie, who did all the inside work on this inquiry. (*He goes to the door*) Well, I'll be getting off to my bed. I'll have a long lie-in in the morning if you don't mind. Come on, Nellie. Up the wooden hills.

Everybody looks round for Nellie. Finally Hedwig steps forward

Hedwig Coming, Bill. Good-night, everyone. Auf Wiedersehen.
Bill You can drop the phoney accent now, dear.
Hedwig Well, thank gawd for that. It was gettin' on me bleedin' wick.
Bill (*opening the door*) Good-night, all.
Hedwig Good-night, dears.

Bill and Hedwig go out

The door closes and the others stare at it without moving as—

the CURTAIN *slowly falls*

FURNITURE AND PROPERTY LIST

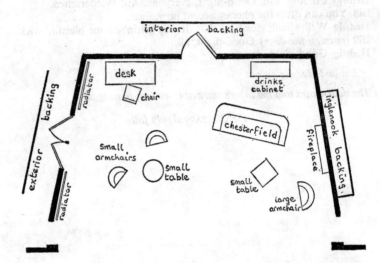

ACT I

SCENE 1

On stage: Chesterfield. *On it:* cushions
Large armchair
Small table DL
2 small armchairs
Small table DR. *On it:* crystal vase containing water and roses
Drinks cabinet. *On it:* Spode-type china ornaments etc. *In it:* glasses, various bottles of drink including sherry, lemonade, lager, 2 bottles of brandy (1 full and 1 opened)
Desk. *On it:* telephone, china ornaments, etc. *In top right-hand drawer:* small blue-leather box containing several letters on white and violet notepaper. *In lower right-hand drawer:* pair of binoculars. *In other drawers:* various typewritten papers and documents
Central-heating radiators R
Pair of silver candlesticks on mantelshelf
Paintings

Off stage: Sprigs of pink may blossom **(Hedwig)**
Vacuum cleaner **(Bethany)**

Personal: **Bethany:** apron

Scene 2

Strike: Used glasses, replace clean ones in the drinks cabinet

Off stage: Bunch of flowers **(Kitty)**

Personal: **Ted:** jeweller's glass in pocket
Patrick: pipe and tobacco, box of matches in jacket pocket

ACT II

On stage: As before except:
On small table DR: tray containing six coffee cups and saucers, sugar
bowl, milk jug, pot of coffee

Off stage: Tray with pot of coffee **(Hedwig)**
Bunch of flowers **(Bill)**

Personal: **Patrick:** box of matches in pocket
Bill: pocket diary, wristwatch, rucksack containing a hammer and
crowbar

LIGHTING PLOT

Practical fittings required: wall brackets
Interior. The same scene throughout

ACT I, SCENE 1.   Mid-afternoon

To open: General, bright sunshine effect
No cues

ACT I, SCENE 2.   Evening

To open: Early evening sunshine effect
No cues

ACT II.   Night

To open: Practicals on, general interior lighting with moonlight effect through
            french windows
No cues

EFFECTS PLOT

MADE AND PRINTED IN GREAT BRITAIN BY
LATIMER TREND & COMPANY LTD PLYMOUTH
MADE IN ENGLAND

EFFECTS PLOT

Cue 1   Melanie runs into the garden   (Page)
         Telephone rings

Cue 2   Heather: "... does he mean by this?"   (Page 7)
         Telephone rings

Cue 3   Philip: "... We couldn't afford it."   (Page 10)
         Telephone rings

Cue 4   before "Oh." ... brings   (Page 30)
         Doorbell rings

Cue 5   ... strikes mantel ... doorbell   (P. 10)
         Doorbell rings

Cue 6   Bill: Cool ... Pauline comes down   (Page 5)
         Final curtain

MADE AND PRINTED IN GREAT BRITAIN BY
LATIMER TREND & COMPANY LTD PLYMOUTH
MADE IN ENGLAND